ISSUES THAT CONCERN YOU

Drunk Driving

Amanda Hiber, *Book Editor*

GREENHAVEN PRESS

A part of Gale, Cengage Learning

GALE
CENGAGE Learning·

Detroit • New York • San Francisco • New Haven, Conn • Waterville, Maine • London

Elizabeth Des Chenes, *Director, Publishing Solutions*

© 2013 Greenhaven Press, a part of Gale, Cengage Learning

Gale and Greenhaven Press are registered trademarks used herein under license.

For more information, contact:
Greenhaven Press
27500 Drake Rd.
Farmington Hills, MI 48331-3535
Or you can visit our Internet site at gale.cengage.com

For product information and technology assistance, contact us at

Gale Customer Support, 1-800-877-4253
For permission to use material from this text or product, submit all requests online at www.cengage.com/permissions

Further permissions questions can be e-mailed to permissionrequest@cengage.com

Articles in Greenhaven Press anthologies are often edited for length to meet page requirements. In addition, original titles of these works are changed to clearly present the main thesis and to explicitly indicate the author's opinion. Every effort is made to ensure that Greenhaven Press accurately reflects the original intent of the authors. Every effort has been made to trace the owners of copyrighted material.

Cover image © Nikola Bilic/Shutterstock.com.

LIBRARY OF CONGRESS CATALOGING-IN-PUBLICATION DATA

Drunk driving / Amanda Hiber, book editor.
    pages cm. -- (Issues that concern you)
 Includes bibliographical references and index.
 ISBN 978-0-7377-6291-4 (hardcover)
 1. Drunk driving--United States. I. Hiber, Amanda.
 HE5620.D72D7817 2013
 363.12'5140973--dc23

                                                2012045146

Printed in the United States of America
1 2 3 4 5 6 7 17 16 15 14 13

CONTENTS

The issue of drunk driving is such a familiar part of America's cultural landscape that it is hard to imagine a time when this was not so. It seems almost inconceivable that not long ago, drunk driving was a fairly socially acceptable facet of American life, and of Western life in general. In 1897 a London taxi driver became the first person ever arrested for drunk driving, and this came after he had driven his cab into a building! In the United States, New York State enacted the first laws against operating a motor vehicle under the influence of alcohol in 1910. But even after this legislation took effect, driving while drunk did not prompt the moral outrage that it does today. "Before the 1980s," says Mothers Against Drunk Driving (MADD) chief executive officer Chuck Hurley, "drinking and driving was how people got home. It was normal behavior."

Even when drunk driving resulted in an accident—and a fatal one at that—public reaction was still so tame as to be unrecognizable today. In his book *One for the Road: Drunk Driving Since 1900*, Barron H. Lerner writes about the first high-profile drunk driving death in the United States, that of *Gone with the Wind* author Margaret Mitchell, who was killed by a drunk driver while walking across the street in 1949. In a National Public Radio interview, Lerner says, "For years and years, back in that era, people who were killed or victimized by a drunk driver were seen as being in the wrong place at the wrong time—that these things happen. And that was very much the case with Margaret Mitchell. After the initial outrage, people started to say, 'Well, it was her time to go.'"

American attitudes toward drunk driving began to shift in the early 1980s. Most sources attribute this shift, in part, to the launching of MADD. Candy Lightner founded this organization in 1980 after her thirteen-year-old daughter was killed by a drunk driver while walking home from a school event. The driver who hit her had been convicted of drunk driving three times in the past and was out on bail from a hit-and-run arrest only two days prior. MADD proved to be highly effective in changing social perceptions of drunk driving. By 1992 a Gallup survey reported that Americans considered drunk driving the number one problem on the nation's highways. Even more than its power to change attitudes, though, was MADD's ability to influence drunk driving legislation.

One of the first major legislative changes concerning drunk driving that MADD heavily advocated for was raising the minimum legal drinking age (MLDA) to twenty-one. After Prohibition, most states' MLDA was twenty-one. But in the early 1970s, states began lowering the age, in keeping with the legal age to vote and enlist in the military. Confronted with rising traffic fatalities among young people, several states raised their MLDAs back up to twenty-one starting in 1976. But groups such as MADD wanted to mandate that all states raise their MLDAs. Finally, in 1984, under pressure from MADD and other groups, President Ronald Reagan signed the National Minimum Drinking Age Act, which threatened to reduce federal transportation funding to states that did not raise their MLDA. By 1987 every state had an MLDA of twenty-one.

Another major change in drunk driving law advocated by MADD was the lowering of the legal blood alcohol concentration (BAC) limit to 0.08 percent. Before legislative change at the federal level, many states did not consider driving illegal unless the driver had a BAC of 0.10 percent or higher. MADD began pushing states to lower their thresholds to 0.08 percent in 1984. As with the MLDA fight, many states lowered their BAC limits voluntarily. Still, as recently as 2000, more states (thirty) had 0.10 percent limits than had 0.08 percent limits (twenty). In October of that year, President Bill Clinton signed a bill that required states to adopt the 0.08 percent BAC limit by 2004 or lose federal transportation funding. All states had MLDAs of twenty-one by 2005.

MADD and other activist groups credit legislative milestones like these with the substantial decrease in drunk driving that has occurred since the 1980s. And, indeed, the contrast is impressive: In 1982 there were 26,173 alcohol-related automobile fatali-

Mothers Against Drunk Driving (MADD) was formed in the early 1980s. MADD heavily lobbied to raise the minimum drinking age to twenty-one.

ties in the United States, and in 2009 there were only 12,744. Still, some say that this analysis is overly simple and that there have been many other factors in play in those years besides the strengthening of drunk driving laws. John McCardell, a former Middlebury College president, launched the organization Choose Responsibility in 2007 with the aim of lowering the MLDA back to eighteen and encouraging young people who use alcohol to do so responsibly. On its website, Choose Responsibility notes: "Motor vehicles are in general much safer now than they were in

1982, when, for example, air bags were rare and crash-worthiness was an unknown term. Drivers are in general better protected, owing not only to these safety features but also to mandatory seatbelt laws." Surely these changes have impacted the decrease in drunk driving fatalities as well, they say.

The debates over the legal drinking age and BAC limits are among many within the larger issue of drunk driving. While all sides clearly desire the same outcome—the eradication of drunk driving—there is a wide array of opinions concerning the most effective means of achieving it. The authors in this volume, *Issues That Concern You: Drunk Driving,* represent this diversity of viewpoints on this substantial social problem. In addition, the book includes several appendices designed to help those interested in the issue learn more about it, including a bibliography for further reading and a list of relevant organizations to contact. The appendix "What You Should Know About Drunk Driving" lists important facts about the scope of the problem and its impact on society. The appendix "What You Should Do About Drunk Driving" provides guidance for students interested in contributing to the fight to end drunk driving. These resources, in addition to the viewpoints included in the book, offer a comprehensive and user-friendly introduction to the issue of drunk driving.

ONE

Drunk Driving Laws Need to Be Tougher

Milwaukee Journal Sentinel

In this viewpoint members of the *Milwaukee Journal Sentinel*'s editorial board discusses several drunk driving bills debated by the Wisconsin Assembly and Senate in 2009, and the authors ultimately argue that tougher laws are needed. Wisconsin has a deeply embedded drinking culture and, consequently, lax drunk driving laws relative to other states. Lawmakers' reluctance to pass stricter laws seems to stem from public reaction, but current laws have cost the state an excessive number of lives and revenue. The authors argue that taking the state's drunk driving problem seriously would require making the first drunk driving offense at least a misdemeanor and the third offense a felony, increasing alcohol taxes, and putting in place sobriety checkpoints.

Politics has been said to be the art of compromise. This supposes that compromise isn't an exercise in minimums.

As the [Wisconsin] state Assembly and Senate reconcile bills on drunken driving reform, it is not at all certain that the argument for saving the most lives possible has been made strongly enough in those chambers.

It is as if legislators started at what the beverage industry, the Tavern League of Wisconsin [a trade group representing alcohol retailers] and legislative leadership might tolerate and then whittled from there—foolishly supposing that the state's drinking public will rise up as one if tougher laws are enacted or new taxes on alcohol are imposed.

Understand, in a state with drunken driving laws as notoriously lax as Wisconsin's, any toughening of these laws is an improvement. But more reform will save more lives.

The Legislature must do more to reform Wisconsin's drunken driving laws. There's still time.

The [*Milwaukee*] *Journal Sentinel's* "Wasted in Wisconsin" series last year [2008] detailed Wisconsin's culture of drinking, a culture enabled by statute. This mind-set has contributed to injury and loss of life on the state's roads and is burdening us all with $2.7 billion in annual costs, including for police, courts, jail and prison.

The series laid out the problem and, admirably, the state Legislature responded. But, taking nothing away from the sponsors of these measures, what has been left on the table is nothing short of astonishing.

This Editorial Board has argued that the third drunken driving offense should be a felony, itself a compromise from an initial call to make the second offense a felony. Currently, it's not a felony until the fifth offense. The Assembly and Senate are likely to agree that the fourth offense should be a felony.

OK, four is between three and five, a compromise. But both the Assembly and Senate also are likely to agree that this will be a felony *only if it occurs within five years of the previous offense.*

Wrong answer. It should be a felony on the third offense—period. And if the Legislature sticks with that fourth offense as a felony, it should be without a five-year caveat.

Even second chances seem permissive given the carnage and collateral damage being inflicted by alcohol abuse. But third chances—and perhaps even more because the offender is past an artificial statute of limitations—is asking too much. This supposes that every single time a driver gets behind the wheel drunk, he or she doesn't put lives at risk. It supposes that somehow the first

© Phil Hands, Wisconsin State Journal.

time is less dangerous than the second or the third or the fourth. . . . And five years separating offenses doesn't make any of them less dangerous.

The message is that state government simply isn't serious enough about the perils of drinking and driving—a message brought home by the Legislature's refusal to consider criminalizing even the first drunken driving offense.

Wisconsin is the only state to treat a first offense much like a traffic offense. It should at least be a misdemeanor. This "first time" in all likelihood isn't the first time this driver has driven drunk.

Cost is said to be the main impediment to tougher enforcement, which will mean more people in the system and more costs for arrests, incarceration, prosecution and treatment. But the cost argument would be more credible if the Legislature was not ignoring a natural revenue source. That would be increased taxes on the substances that make the reform necessary.

The state's beer tax—at $2 per barrel—is the third-lowest in the nation and has been untouched for 40 years. [Since 1969]

Wisconsin's excise tax on wine is among the lowest in the nation and, for distilled spirits, the state is in about the middle of the pack among the 32 states and the District of Columbia that have such a tax.

A bill by Rep. Terese Berceau (D-Madison) to increase the beer tax to $10 per barrel has gotten a hearing but is not given much of a shot at passage. And no one seems to be talking about a tax on wine. Spirits are being discussed as a revenue source, but only by the Senate. The Assembly is balking.

Legislators should not use public unwillingness to pay as the cause for their reluctance on taxes. A survey by University of Wisconsin Health earlier this year [2009] showed nearly 60%

Wisconsin governor Jim Doyle signs legislation in 2003 that lowers the legal blood alcohol concentration for Wisconsin drivers from 0.10 to 0.08.

of Wisconsinites approved of an increase in the beer tax if the money is used for treatment or law enforcement involving alcohol abuse. Citizens would understand that taxes on wine and spirits are necessary as well.

One stated fear is that a governor would raid these "designated" funds for non-designated uses. We've long criticized this practice, but using it as a reason to oppose creating a new revenue source is an argument that blocks virtually any initiative that requires new funding.

Another possibility that has been ignored: Sobriety checkpoints [roadblocks where police check drivers' sobriety]. They are allowed in 38 other states but prohibited in Wisconsin. The arguments against these usually center on efficacy and privacy.

They do take some drunken drivers off the road but, in truth, their value is in keeping them off the road in the first place. They are an effective deterrent. Told that sobriety checkpoints will be set up, drivers think hard before tanking up.

The U.S. Supreme Court has undercut the privacy argument, ruling in 1990 that "minimally intrusive" checkpoints are permissible. But we suspect these privacy arguments, as with much of the opposition to reforms, are simple cover for anxiety about more checks generally against drivers who drink. That anxiety likely stems from worries that even moderate drinking will get drivers in trouble. No. We don't encourage *any* drinking and driving, but the 0.08% blood-alcohol threshold will continue to be the limit that triggers enforcement.

Another diluted proposal: Legislators are considering making the first offense a misdemeanor if a child is in the car. Want to be tough? Make that a felony and *all* first offenses a misdemeanor.

Rep. Josh Zepnick (D-Milwaukee), who lost a sister to a drunken driver, has proposed bills that would mandate absolute sobriety from bartenders on the job and would ban all-you-can-drink specials. The rationale: Drunk bartenders are in no position to determine if they are over-serving customers, and drink specials encourage a lot of drinking in a short period, a recipe for drunken driving.

Zepnick said he is willing to negotiate to accommodate reasonable concerns, but even so, these common-sense measures are given little chance of success.

Toughened drunken driving laws of the kind now being considered will save lives and help reverse Wisconsin's image as a state of hard-core bingers. But fear of entrenched interests and flawed perceptions about the public's reaction is producing far too little.

Compromise seems to have been the default position. Necessity—and saving the maximum number of lives possible—would have been a far better starting point. But there's still time to do more. The Legislature should make the effort.

TWO

MADD Gets Madder

Eric Peters

In this viewpoint automotive columnist and author Eric Peters argues that drunk driving laws have become unreasonable, with no real evidence of their necessity. Peters places the blame for unfounded laws primarily on the organization Mothers Against Drunk Driving (MADD), which he says targets drinking in general, not just drinking and driving. He argues that MADD has attached a stigma to social drinking, when in reality it is drivers who drink in excess that cause most alcohol-related accidents. Thus, according to Peters, current drunk driving laws are ineffective in addition to being unreasonable.

I don't support drunk driving—just to get that out of the way. But the idea that you're "drunk" at the current .08 BAC concentration threshold is a bit much.

Push them a bit and proponents will say you're *impaired* at .08 in terms of a medically observable decline in reaction times—and that's true, as far as it goes. But this slight reduction in reaction times has not been shown to correlate with a higher accident rate.

Proponents merely *assert* that it does, with no facts (such as a greater number of car wrecks) to back it up.

A woman takes a Breathalyzer test to check her blood alcohol concentration (BAC). Critics of drunk driving laws say that lowering the legal BAC does not lower the accident rate.

On the other hand, we know that a .10 BAC, which used to be the legal threshold defining drunk driving in most states, *does* correlate with a higher accident rate. There is actual evidence (more car crashes) to support this. Therefore, it seems reasonable to target people with BAC levels at .10 or higher because they pose an objective, real threat to other motorists (and pedestrians).

That's what the system used to do. The BAC threshold defining "drunk driving" used to be .10—because that was the level at which it was known drivers tended to have more accidents.

Not anymore. The lawful maximum BAC nationwide is now .08 and threatens to get knocked down even lower. In many states, you can be arrested for DUI with a BAC level of .06. "Zero tolerance"—that is, no alcohol whatsoever, is openly discussed.

Which is just silly. Do we really believe people ought to be arrested because they got behind the wheel of a car after having had a *sip* of wine?

So, how did we get from reasonable DWI laws to here—objectively *unreasonable* DWI laws that target social drinkers with even very moderate amounts of alcohol in their systems with a vengefulness that borders on the pathological?

All it took was one "mom."

MADD—Mothers Against Drunk Driving—has built a mighty empire in the pursuit of latter-day Prohibition. It is today one of the largest, best-funded, most aggressive political lobbies in the country.

MADD employs a large staff of full-time employees, has highly-paid executives and takes in millions of dollars annually. Lawmakers from the city council level all the way up dread being targeted by MADD and so bend over backwards to support whatever measure MADD puts forward. Do otherwise and, *clearly*, you must be a supporter of drunk driving.

Launched in the 1980s as a true grassroots movement, MADD has become another D.C. special interest. And its special interest is outlawing any alcohol consumption—or as close to that as possible.

MADD has gone on record advocating that lawful BAC maximums be lowered to as little as .04—a level the average-weight person can reach after consuming a single beer or glass of wine. The organization wants to see people hauled out of their cars and cuffed and stuffed over this.

Which isn't MADD.

It's *insane*.

The twisted thing MADD has managed to achieve is more or less the same thing that "civil rights" groups have achieved vis-à-vis racial set-asides and preferential treatment. Have the temerity to suggest that consuming any alcohol at all prior to driving—no matter how little—isn't necessarily bad let alone criminal, and you're in favor of "drunk driving."

Just as criticizing affirmative action guarantees catcalls of "racism" from the civil rights industry.

This isn't argument—it's *intimidation*. Which is what demagogues do when they can't debate the facts.

And the facts are not on MADD's side.

First, there's the fact that the War on Drunk Driving . . . was won long ago. There is now enormous social stigma associated with driving drunk—*really* drunk. In the '60s and '70s middle and upper class people did it often—cheerfully. One for the road!

Nowadays, it's anathema to climb into a car after a night of boozing it up. It's just not done.

Or not done *much*.

Very few people (the minority of repeat offending, "problem drinkers" aside) get behind the wheel of a car after having had more than a drink or two—which is what *most* people do when they go out for dinner, say, after work.

There's the social stigma—and there's the prospect of potentially career-ending/life-changing punishment for being convicted of drunk driving.

So most people self-regulate—or they call or cab.

Second, there's the fact that it's drivers with BAC levels of .10 or above who constitute the problem—insofar as having *accidents* goes. Constantly lowering the lawful maximum BAC level doesn't do anything except turn social drinkers into "drunks" by the arbitrary stroke of a lawmaker's pen. It's exactly like having speed limits that are set so low that virtually every driver on the road is technically guilty of "speeding." No harm's being done—but more and more people are now in the crosshairs of law-enforcement.

Courtesy of MADD.

Meanwhile, the aggressiveness of enforcement—"sobriety checkpoints"—continues to step up, even though these check-

No Significant Fatality Drop from .08 BAC (Blood Alcohol Concentration) Alone Laws

Results of the 11-State Study of .08 BAC Laws

State	Year .08 BAC law became effective	Statistically significant reduction occurred in:		
		Alcohol-related fatalities	Fatalities involving "high BAC" drivers	Proportion of fatalities involving "high BAC" drivers to those involving sober drivers
Utah	1983	No	No	No
Oregon	1983	No	No	No
Maine	1988	No	No	No
California	1990	No	No	No
Vermont	1991	**Yes**	**Yes**	**Yes**
Kansas	1993	No	No	**Yes**
North Carolina	1993	No	No	**Yes**
Florida	1994	**Yes**	**Yes**	**Yes**
New Hampshire	1994	No	No	No
New Mexico	1994	No	No	**Yes**
Virginia	1994	No	No	No
Total		**2 of 11**	**2 of 11**	**5 of 11**

Note: "Yes" indicates a statistically significant reduction after the .08 BAC law became effective. "No" indicates no statistically significant reduction.

Taken from: U.S.G.A.O. Report to Congressional Committees: Highway Safety: Effectiveness of State .08 Blood Alcohol Laws, June 1999. www.abionline.org.

points are lousy at sussing out the real drunks, the drivers with BAC levels of .10 or higher. While the cops spend hours at these checkpoints depriving masses of drivers of their Fourth and Fifth Amendment rights trying to ferret out some poor schmuck who had two beers over dinner and isn't a threat to anyone, the *pro*—the guy with a BAC level in the double digits—enjoys an enhanced probability of escaping attention simply because there are fewer cops out patrolling the roads. And it is out on the road that one can best find the pros—because their driving is actually impaired and thus *noticeable*.

Pros weave and cross over the double yellow; they drive on the shoulder—and the wrong way up exit ramps.

Because, after all, they are *drunk*.

And, it shows.

That's how the authorities used to ID them. It worked well.

It could work again, too.

But our current DWI laws—and MADD, which is largely responsible for them—aren't designed to be effective, or rather, *reasonable*. They're designed to target people whose only manifestation of being "drunk" is registering an arbitrary and ever-lower BAC number on a machine. They don't weave or otherwise drive erratically. And they don't get into accidents. (If anything, most people with minor amounts of alcohol in their systems drive more carefully, both to compensate and out of fear of being involved in an accident.)

They'd go unnoticed and probably make it home without incident were it not for all these sobriety dragnets.

But none of this matters to MADD.

All that matters is the cause—and the sense of mission (and the money and the political power) that comes along for the ride.

I could sure use a drink. . . .

THREE

Drunk Driving Laws Should Focus on Impairment, Not Alcohol Use

Radley Balko

In the following viewpoint Radley Balko, senior editor at *Reason* magazine, questions current drunk driving laws that rely solely on blood alcohol concentration (BAC) to determine a driver's impairment level. The problem with this approach, he says, is that people react differently to different amounts of alcohol; one person may be impaired at a certain BAC level while someone else may not be. Balko proposes abolishing drunk driving laws completely. He cites evidence that the 2000 federal law encouraging states to lower their BAC thresholds from 0.10 to 0.08 actually resulted in more traffic fatalities because it shifted the focus away from excessively drunk drivers. The threat of drunk driving lies in the impairment caused by drinking, not in drinking itself, says Balko. In order to improve traffic safety, laws should punish reckless driving, whether it is caused by drinking or other distractions.

Last week [October 2010] Austin [Texas] Police Chief Art Acevedo advocated creating a new criminal offense: "driving while ability impaired." The problem with the current Texas law prohibiting "driving while intoxicated" (DWI), Acevedo explained, is that it doesn't allow him to arrest a driver whose blood-alcohol content (BAC) is below 0.08 percent without additional evidence of impairment.

"People sometimes focus on how many drinks they can have before they'll go to jail," Acevedo told the *Austin-American Statesman*. "It varies. . . . A person may be intoxicated at 0.05, and you don't want them out driving." Acevedo wants to be able to arrest people with BAC levels as low as 0.05 percent, and he may have support for that idea in the state legislature. John Whitmire (D-Houston), chairman of the state Senate's Criminal Justice Committee, told the *Statesman* Acevedo's plan "might be one way to go," adding, "Some people shouldn't be driving after one drink—probably below the 0.08 limit—and this could address that."

Bill Lewis, head of the Texas chapter of Mothers Against Drunk Driving, agreed. "I don't see how it would hurt," he told the paper. "The level of 0.08 is where we know most people are good and drunk . . . and there are people who are driving at less than the limit who probably should not be. It might keep some people from driving [drunk] again."

Acevedo, Whitmore, and Lewis are right, although probably not in the way they intended. People do react to alcohol differently. For many people one drink may well be too many, while experienced drinkers can function relatively normally with a BAC at or above the legal threshold for presuming intoxication. A person's impairment may also depend on variables such as the medications he is taking and the amount of sleep he got the night before. Acevedo et al.'s objections to the legal definition of intoxication highlight the absurdity of drawing an arbitrary, breathalyzer-based line between sobriety and criminal intoxication.

The right solution, however, is not to push the artificial line back farther. Instead we should get rid of it entirely by repealing drunk driving laws.

Law Had Unintended Effect

Consider the 2000 federal law that pressured states to lower their BAC standards to 0.08 from 0.10. At the time, the average BAC in alcohol-related fatal accidents was 0.17, and two-thirds of such accidents involved drivers with BACs of 0.14 or higher. In fact, drivers with BACs between 0.01 and 0.03 were involved in more fatal accidents than drivers with BACs between 0.08 and 0.10. (The federal government classifies a fatal accident as "alcohol-related" if it involved a driver, a biker, or a pedestrian with a BAC of 0.01 or more, whether or not drinking actually contributed to the accident.) In 1995 the National Highway Traffic Safety Administration studied traffic data in 30 safety categories from the first five states to adopt the new DWI standard. In 21 of the 30 categories, those states were either no different from or less safe than the rest of the country.

Once the 0.08 standard took effect nationwide in 2000, a curious thing happened: Alcohol-related traffic fatalities *increased*, following a 20-year decline. Critics of the 0.08 standard predicted this would happen. The problem is that most people with a BAC between 0.08 and 0.10 don't drive erratically enough to be noticed by police officers in patrol cars. So police began setting up roadblocks to catch them. But every cop manning a roadblock aimed at catching motorists violating the new law is a cop not on the highways looking for more seriously impaired motorists. By 2004 alcohol-related fatalities went down again, but only because the decrease in states that don't use roadblocks compensated for a slight but continuing increase in the states that use them.

A Constitutional Exception?

The roadblocks are also constitutionally problematic. In the 1990 decision *Michigan v. Sitz*, the Supreme Court acknowledged that stops at sobriety checkpoints constitute "seizures" under the Fourth Amendment but ruled that the public safety threat posed by drunk driving made them "reasonable." In the years since, the checkpoints have become little more than revenue generators for local governments. When local newspapers inquire about specific

Alcohol affects people differently. For some people one drink may be too many to drive while others can function fine at the legal limit, reports the author.

roadblocks after the fact, they inevitably find lots of citations for seat belt offenses, broken headlights, driving with an expired license, and other minor infractions. But the checkpoints rarely catch seriously impaired drivers. In 2009, according to a recent study by researchers at the University of California at Berkeley, 1,600 sobriety checkpoints in California generated $40 million in fines, $30 million in overtime pay for cops, 24,000 vehicle confiscations, and just 3,200 arrests for drunk driving. A typical checkpoint would consist of 20 or more cops, yield a dozen or more vehicle confiscations, but around three drunk driving arrests.

Checkpoints are only the beginning of what California DWI attorney Lawrence Taylor calls "the drunk driving exception to the Constitution." The Fifth Amendment right against self-incrimination has been turned upside down by state laws that instantly suspend the licenses of drivers who refuse to take road-side breath tests. Those breath tests are also fraught with problems. Most manufacturers of breath test machines have refused to turn over their source code, meaning DWI defendants can't assess the machines' margin of error, which can be a significant factor in a case where the difference between 0.80 and 0.79 for a first offense can be $1,000 or more in fines, mandatory alcohol awareness classes, and loss of driving privileges for up to a year.

Ever-Expanding Powers

Blood tests are far more accurate, but by the time a driver is pulled over, questioned, taken to the nearest hospital, and had his blood drawn, his BAC may be significantly different from what it was when he was driving. Perversely, the time lapse can have the effect of protecting guiltier motorists. Imagine a driver pulled over or stopped at a checkpoint after having "one for the road," knowing his house is a short drive away and the last drink won't kick in until he's sitting on his couch. At the time he is stopped, he is under the legal limit. But his BAC is rising, and it tops 0.08 by the time his blood is drawn at the hospital. By contrast, a driver who is impaired when he's pulled over, but who stopped drinking an hour or so before, benefits from the delay, since his BAC is falling by the time he arrives at the hospital.

Many states have tried to solve this problem by claiming another invasive power: They are now allowing police to forcibly take a blood sample on the side of the road.

These ever-expanding enforcement powers miss the point: The threat posed by drunk driving comes not from drinking per se but from the impairment drinking can cause. That fact has been lost in the rush to demonize people who have even a single drink before getting behind the wheel (exemplified by the shift in the government's message from "Don't Drive Drunk" to "Don't Drink and Drive"). Several studies have found that talking on a cell phone, even with a hands-free device, causes more driver impairment than a 0.08 BAC. A 2001 American Automobile Association study found several other in-car distractions that also caused more impairment, including eating, adjusting a radio or CD player, and having kids in the backseat. . . .

Focus on Impairment

If our ultimate goals are to reduce driver impairment and maximize highway safety, we should be punishing reckless driving. It shouldn't matter if it's caused by alcohol, sleep deprivation, prescription medication, text messaging, or road rage. If lawmakers want to stick it to dangerous drivers who threaten everyone else on the road, they can dial up the civil and criminal liability for reckless driving, especially in cases that result in injury or property damage.

Doing away with the specific charge of drunk driving sounds radical at first blush, but it would put the focus back on impairment, where it belongs. It might repair some of the civil-liberties damage done by the invasive powers the government says it needs to catch and convict drunk drivers. If the offense were reckless driving rather than drunk driving, for example, repeated swerving over the median line would be enough to justify the charge. There would be no need for a cop to jam a needle in your arm alongside a busy highway.

Scrapping the DWI offense in favor of better enforcement of reckless driving laws would also bring some logical consistency to our laws, which treat a driver with a BAC of 0.08 much more harshly than, say, a driver distracted by his kids or a cell phone call, despite similar levels of impairment. The punishable act should be violating road rules or causing an accident, not the factors that led to those offenses. Singling out alcohol impairment for extra punishment isn't about making the roads safer. It's about a lingering hostility toward demon rum [a term used during Prohibition to refer to alcohol].

FOUR

Anonymous Tips Should Be Used to Prevent Drunk Driving

John Roberts

In the following viewpoint US Supreme Court chief justice John Roberts offers his dissenting opinion in the Supreme Court's decision to not review the 2009 *Virginia v. Harris* case, which involved a driver, Joseph Harris, who was arrested and convicted of driving while intoxicated. Harris's arrest was based on an anonymous tip and the arresting officer's observations of Harris's behavior, but because the officer did not verify on his own that Harris was driving dangerously, the Virginia Supreme Court overturned the conviction. Seven US Supreme Court justices voted not to review this decision, while Justices Antonin Scalia and Roberts disagreed with the majority. Roberts argues here that although the Fourth Amendment may pose legitimate challenges to some convictions, drunk driving cases pose unique dangers and thus require different standards. Ultimately, Roberts argues, protecting drunk driving suspects' questionable constitutional rights should not take precedence over protecting innocent lives. Thus, law enforcement's ability to lawfully prevent drunk driving should not be limited.

John Roberts, "Dissenting Opinion, Virginia v. Harris," Supremecourt.gov, October 20, 2009.

Every year, close to 13,000 people die in alcohol-related car crashes—roughly one death every 40 minutes. Ordinary citizens are well aware of the dangers posed by drunk driving, and they frequently report such conduct to the police. A number of States have adopted programs specifically designed to encourage such tips—programs such as the "Drunkbusters Hotline" in New Mexico and the REDDI program (Report Every Drunk Driver Immediately) in force in several States.

By a 4-to-3 vote, the Virginia Supreme Court adopted a rule that will undermine such efforts to get drunk drivers off the road. The decision . . . commands that police officers following a driver reported to be drunk *do nothing* until they see the driver actually do something unsafe on the road—by which time it may be too late.

A Richmond police officer pulled Joseph Harris over after receiving an anonymous tip that Harris was driving while intoxicated. The tip described Harris, his car, and the direction he was traveling in considerable detail. The officer did not personally witness Harris violate any traffic laws. When Harris was pulled over, however, he reeked of alcohol, his speech was slurred, he almost fell over in attempting to exit his car, and he failed the sobriety tests the officer administered on the scene. Harris was convicted of driving while intoxicated, but the Virginia Supreme Court overturned the conviction. It concluded that because the officer had failed to independently verify that Harris was driving dangerously, the stop violated the Fourth Amendment's prohibition on unreasonable searches and seizures.

I am not sure that the Fourth Amendment requires such independent corroboration before the police can act, at least in the special context of anonymous tips reporting drunk driving. This is an important question that is not answered by our past decisions, and that has deeply divided federal and state courts. The Court should grant the petition for certiorari [an order to a lower court to submit all case documents for the higher court's review] to answer the question and resolve the conflict.

Not a Clear Precedent

On the one hand, our cases allow police to conduct investigative stops based on reasonable suspicion, viewed under the totality of the circumstances. In *Florida v. J. L.* (2000), however, we [the Supreme Court] explained that anonymous tips, in the absence of additional corroboration, typically lack the "indicia of reliability" needed to justify a stop under the reasonable suspicion standard.

Chief Justice of the United States John Roberts believes that while the Fourth Amendment poses legitimate challenges to some drunk driving cases, the safety of innocent people should take precedence over the dubious rights of drunk drivers.

In *J. L.*, the Court suppressed evidence seized by police after receiving an anonymous tip alleging that a young man, wearing a plaid shirt and waiting at a particular bus stop, was carrying a gun. The majority . . . relied extensively on *J. L.* in reversing Harris's conviction.

But it is not clear that *J. L.* applies to anonymous tips reporting drunk or erratic driving. *J. L.* itself suggested that the Fourth Amendment analysis might be different in other situations. The Court declined "to speculate about the circumstances under which the danger alleged in an anonymous tip might be so great as to justify a search even without a showing of reliability." It also hinted that "in quarters where the reasonable expectation of Fourth Amendment privacy is diminished," it might be constitutionally permissible to "conduct protective searches on the basis of information insufficient to justify searches elsewhere.". . .

There is no question that drunk driving is a serious and potentially deadly crime, as our cases have repeatedly emphasized. The imminence of the danger posed by drunk drivers exceeds that at issue in other types of cases. In a case like *J. L.*, the police can often observe the subject of a tip and step in before actual harm occurs; with drunk driving, such a wait-and-see approach may prove fatal. Drunk driving is always dangerous, as it is occurring. This Court has in fact recognized that the dangers posed by drunk drivers are unique, frequently upholding anti-drunk-driving policies that might be constitutionally problematic in other, less exigent circumstances.

Stakes Are High

In the absence of controlling precedent on point, a sharp disagreement has emerged among federal and state courts over how to apply the Fourth Amendment in this context. The majority of courts examining the question have upheld investigative stops of allegedly drunk or erratic drivers, even when the police did not personally witness any traffic violations before conducting the stops. These courts have typically distinguished *J. L.*'s general rule

Average reaction times, in seconds, at 35 miles per hour

Average reaction times, in seconds, at 70 miles per hour

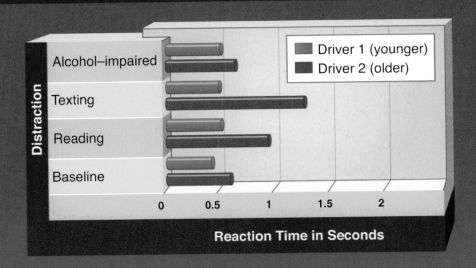

Taken from: Graphs based on data from "Texting While Driving. How Dangerous Is It?" *Car and Driver*, June 2009.
http://caranddriver.com.

based on some combination of (1) the especially grave and imminent dangers posed by drunk driving; (2) the enhanced reliability of tips alleging illegal activity in public, to which the tipster was presumably an eyewitness; (3) the fact that traffic stops are typically less invasive than searches or seizures of individuals on foot; and (4) the diminished expectation of privacy enjoyed by individuals driving their cars on public roads. A minority of jurisdictions, meanwhile, take the same position as the Virginia Supreme Court, requiring that officers first confirm an anonymous tip of drunk or erratic driving through their own independent observation. This conflict has been expressly noted by the lower courts.

The conflict is clear and the stakes are high. The effect of the rule . . . will be to grant drunk drivers "one free swerve" before they can legally be pulled over by police. It will be difficult for an officer to explain to the family of a motorist killed by that swerve that the police had a tip that the driver of the other car was drunk, but that they were powerless to pull him over, even for a quick check.

Maybe the decision of the Virginia Supreme Court was correct, and the Fourth Amendment bars police from acting on anonymous tips of drunk driving unless they can verify each tip. If so, then the dangerous consequences of this rule are unavoidable. But the police should have every legitimate tool at their disposal for getting drunk drivers off the road. I would grant certiorari to determine if this is one of them.

FIVE

Undocumented Immigrants Are a Large Portion of Drunk Drivers

R. Cort Kirkwood

> R. Cort Kirkwood is managing editor of the *Daily News-Record* in Harrisonburg, Virginia, and has written articles for the *Christian Science Monitor*, *National Review*, and other publications. In the viewpoint below Kirkwood says that a disproportionate number of drunk drivers are undocumented immigrants. He cites evidence that those states with the highest numbers of undocumented immigrants are the same states with the highest numbers of both fatal hit-and-run car accidents and fatal crashes involving unlicensed drivers. Kirkwood says most of the drivers involved in such accidents are Hispanics—and in particular, Mexicans—who come from a culture that encourages heavy drinking and takes drinking and driving less seriously than American culture.

The Ceran family of Salt Lake City, Utah, was returning home on Christmas Eve [2006] after attending a performance of *A Christmas Carol*. They didn't know who awaited them on the road: Carlos Rodolfo Prieto, an unlicensed, drunk-driving illegal alien from Mexico. The 24-year-old Prieto, prosecutors allege, ran a red light and smashed into the six Cerans, killing Cheryl Ceran, 47, and two of her children, 15-year-old Ian and 7-year-old Julianna. Gary Ceran, 45, and two other children survived the crash.

So did Prieto. He failed a roadside sobriety test and confessed to drinking five beers before the rubber hit the road. Police had collared Prieto twice before for DUI [driving under the influence]. He was not deported.

In October [2006], an illegal alien admitted drinking a 12-pack of beer before he killed someone in Tennessee. And in two weeks alone over late October and early November [2006], World Net Daily [WND] has reported, drunk-driving illegals killed five people in North Carolina.

Highway homicide is a deadly and largely unknown aspect of illegal immigration, and startling data and horror stories from newspapers across the country show that the states with the highest numbers of illegals are, most likely, the most dangerous places to drive.

Higher Hit-and-Run Accidents

One such eye-opener appeared as "The hit-kill-and-run state" stories, published in 2005 in the *Arizona Daily Star*. "The seven states with the highest rates of fatal hit-and-run crashes," the paper reported, "are also the seven states that have the most illegal immigrants, according to two think tanks." With 500,000 illegal aliens, or 9 percent of its population, the paper reported, Arizona ranked fifth in that measure behind California, Texas, Florida, and New York. About 5.6 percent of Arizona's fatal crashes between 1994 and 2004, the newspaper reported, were hit-and-run.

In California, the state with the most illegal immigrants, more than 7 percent of the fatal wrecks were hit-and-run, the *Daily Star* reported, the highest in the nation. With one million unlicensed drivers, California also boasted the highest number of hit-and-runs of all the states, according to a 2003 *San Francisco Chronicle* article.

More recent data on California, gleaned from the federal Fatality Analysis Reporting System, show that California's figure for fatal hit-and-runs in 2005 reached 9 percent, or 347 of 3,846 fatal crashes. Arizona's number stayed the same as its average from 1994 to 2004. The figure for Texas came in at 5 percent, an increase from 4.5 percent. Florida's figure increased from 4.9 percent to 5.6 percent.

By contrast, the states with the lowest percentage of fatal hit-and-run crashes also had the lowest number of illegals. In Vermont, with 4,000 illegals in 2005, the Federation for American Immigration Reform reports, one of 68 fatal crashes was a hit-and-run. Wyoming, also with 4,000 illegals, posted just one hit-and-run fatality among 147 total, or 0.6 percent. Maine too had just 4,000 illegals. Just one of its 151 fatal crashes was a hit-and-run.

"A lot of it," a traffic expert told the paper, "is the Mexican border." Indeed it is. And not just for hit-and-run killers.

A Correlation Between Unlicensed and Undocumented

More proof that illegal immigrants are lethal drivers is found in the evidence tying unlicensed drivers, who are disproportionately illegal aliens, to traffic fatalities. The American Automobile Association (AAA) published the second of two reports in 2003 documenting that unlicensed drivers are more lethal than licensed drivers. That report, entitled "Unlicensed to Kill, The Sequel," used numbers gathered between 1993 to 1999. Unsurprisingly, correlating the AAA data with other figures detailing the number of illegal aliens in a state demonstrates that states with the highest numbers of fatal crashes involving unlicensed drivers correspond to the states with the highest numbers of illegal aliens. In California, with the highest population of illegals, at least 20.9 percent of the drivers in fatal crashes were unlicensed. Arizona's and New Mexico's figures were even higher: 21.1 and 23.1. Maine's figure was just 6.1 percent, Wyoming's, 11.2 and Vermont's 13.7.

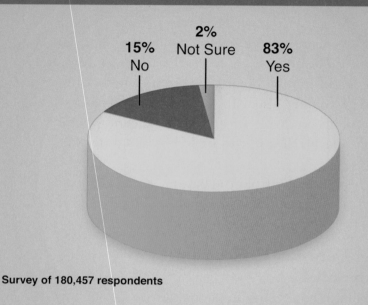

Should police officers be allowed to check the immigration status of every person who is stopped or arrested?

15%
No

2%
Not Sure

83%
Yes

Survey of 180,457 respondents

Taken from: Morgan Skinner. "Police Check Immigration." KCS6 News, June 28, 2012. www.kcsg.com.

Law enforcement authorities confirm that unlicensed drivers are disproportionately illegal aliens. According to World Net Daily, a district attorney in New York has reported that at one point, 66 percent of those charged with misdemeanor unlicensed driving were illegals. "Unfortunately," a highway patrolman in California told WND, "the undocumented drivers here [drive unlicensed] more than the natives." In short, illegal aliens drive without licenses and cause fatalities in numbers exceeding their proportion of the population.

Assuming these data aren't a wild fluke, the obvious question is why illegal aliens, mostly Mexicans, are so often unlicensed, and why they so often leave the scene of an accident. The answers are hardly a mystery. They are unlicensed because they are illegal, although being illegal does not mean they will be unlicensed. . . .

With respect to hit-and-runs, illegals have nothing to gain and everything to lose by hanging around to face the law's mariachi band. If caught, they face deportation, although deportation, as the Cerans and others have learned, is hardly a fait accompli.

"A Cultural Thing"

Yet another pathology among illegal aliens is drunk driving, which explains, in large measure, why illegal aliens are such lethal drivers. Illegal aliens in particular and unassimilated Hispanics in general are often indifferent to drunk-driving laws, thanks to Latin American cultural attitudes, which are more liberal than ours. The repercussions of those attitudes surface in data proving that Hispanics are arrested for drunk driving in numbers exceeding their percentage of the population.

The data and strong anecdotal evidence show that large numbers of Hispanics, particularly Mexicans, are not assimilating American society's norms on drinking and driving, but instead retaining and even celebrating cultural norms and attitudes they carry across the border.

More than one publication has flatly proven, and stated, that culture is the problem when it comes to Hispanics and high arrest rates for drunk driving. In May [2006], the *Record* of Stockton, California, in "DUI's Culture Gap," reported that between 2000–2004, 54 percent of all arrests for drunk driving in Stockton were Hispanic men, although they make up only 35.3 percent of the population. The paper further parsed the data, but you get the idea. Hispanics, the paper reported, accounted for more DUI arrests than any other racial group. The *Record*'s data are nothing new. Overall in California, Mothers Against Drunk Driving reported in 2001, Hispanics accounted for 44.1 percent of DUI arrests but composed just 31.3 percent of the population. California's data comport with those of other states, the *Record* reported, including North Carolina and Texas.

Because Hispanics are arrested for drunk driving in numbers exceeding their proportion of the population, it's hardly a long jump to conclude that many are illegal aliens, but again, illegality does not explain these statistics. *Driven* magazine, published by Mothers Against Drunk Driving, disclosed an unspoken truth in a 2001 article entitled "Cultural Impact": Mexican culture encourages heavy drinking.

Different Attitudes Toward Drunk Driving

The Mexican mother of a four-year-old mangled by a drunk driver explained the problem. "In Mexico," she said, "the culture is very much a drinking culture." Reported the same article, "Hispanic drivers are more likely than Anglo drivers to consume more alcohol more frequently and have been shown to be more likely than Anglos to drive with a blood alcohol concentration (BAC) level over .05 percent. Hispanics also believed that it takes six to eight drinks to affect driving, while Anglos thought two to four drinks affected driving."

In 2003, the *Austin-American Statesman* published an article titled "Hispanics and DUI: A Troubling Trend," revealing similar statistics to those published in the *Stockton Record.* "One thing I have noticed," a cop told the paper, "is that the Hispanics I arrest for DWI [driving while intoxicated], 90 percent of the time, are more drunk than the white and black people I arrest." The paper also quoted a professor at the University of Texas who studied Hispanics and drinking. "The profile of a drunk driver in California," Raul Caetano told the paper, "is a young Hispanic male, and I bet you have a similar situation all over the Southwest." And "the traditional pattern of drinking in Mexico is one of infrequent drinking of high amounts."

The *Record of Stockton* affirmed that truth. "The Latino community creates its own problems," Joe Ynostroza, an expert on Hispanics and alcoholism, told the paper. "The problem is especially acute in Mexico," the paper averred. "Most of this is first- or second-generation Mexican males," Ynostroza said. "Alcoholism runs rampant in the Mexican Latino community."

In the words of one Hispanic cop: "It's a cultural thing."

Microcosm: Virginia's Eastern Shore

"Harvest of Death," published in Norfolk's *Virginian Pilot* in October 2005, put a journalistic microscope on Virginia's Eastern Shore. Hispanic migrants, meaning the illegal aliens who pick tomatoes there, are driving a wave of unprecedented road crime and exemplify all the aforementioned problems.

Hispanics "driving rogue vehicles," the *Pilot* reported, injured 90 persons and killed 18 between 2002 and the time of the newspaper's report. Why the paper used "rogue" to describe the vehicles, instead of the drivers, we can only guess, but "the fatalities represent about one-fourth of the 71 highway deaths on the Eastern Shore in that period." Yet Hispanics are just 5 percent of the population of 51,000. Unsurprisingly, when the number of illegals grows during picking season, so does the number of fatalities.

Carlos Prieto (at right, standing) is arraigned in court for killing three members of the Ceran family in Toole, Utah. Prieto, an undocumented immigrant who had been arrested twice before for drunk driving, had not been deported.

No wonder the 77 miles of the Eastern Shore's U.S. 13, from the Chesapeake Bay Bridge-Tunnel to Maryland, the *Pilot* reported, is "one of the most treacherous highways in Virginia," with a fatality rate in 2003 "more than four times the rates on Interstates 64, 81 and 95 in Virginia."

In only three of the 18 fatal wrecks, the paper reported, did the Hispanic driver have insurance. Other common features in these wrecks? No inspection stickers, no driver's license, and plenty of booze.

Reviewing 179 crash reports from state police involving Hispanic drivers between 2002 and 2004, the paper discovered that 75 percent were uninsured, "more than four times the national rate for uninsured motorists." As well, "nearly all" the Hispanic drivers used cars "registered to other drivers" and 93 percent of the vehicles carried "out-of-state tags—most of them from Tennessee." The paper did not report it, but most of these Hispanics were likely illegal aliens. One cop complained that officials often don't know which embassy to contact after a fatality.

When Will It End?

And when you mention this vehicular rap sheet, the open-borders crowd will complain that illegals "do the jobs Americans won't do." Well, they also do other things most Americans won't do. They drive without licenses or insurance. They hit and run. They drive drunk.

Part of the problem—hit-and-run fatalities and unlicensed, uninsured drivers—is their illegal status. The other part—drunk-driving—is cultural. But another different problem is their causing a backlash against legal immigrants who assimilate, obey the law and become good citizens. They, too, must be aghast.

Whatever the problem, most American policymakers are clearly unconcerned. But maybe when the son or daughter of a congressman or president is tragically killed, they will, at long last, stop illegal immigration. As the Cerans of this country know, Americans face enough homegrown highway hooligans without importing more.

SIX

Laws Targeting Undocumented Drunk Drivers Are Misguided

Chris Burbank

In the following viewpoint Salt Lake City, Utah, police chief Chris Burbank makes a statement before the US House of Representatives Subcommittee on Immigration Policy and Enforcement on the issue of the Scott Gardner Act, which would require the immediate deportation of any undocumented immigrant arrested for drunk driving. In his statement, Burbank asserts the need for effective legislation that would keep repeat drunk drivers off the road. But, he says, there is no valid evidence showing that undocumented immigrants drive drunk more than other drivers, making a drunk driver's citizenship status irrelevant. The Scott Gardner Act, Burbank says, would actually encourage racial profiling by individual officers and place inappropriate burdens on local police departments.

The goal of local law enforcement is to provide for public well-being and security while safeguarding the civil rights of all persons, equally without bias. Proper and effective policing occurs when we profile for criminal behavior, not for race, ethnicity, religion, gender or sexual orientation.

Chris Burbank, "Statement before the Subcommittee on Immigration Policy and Enforcement Hearing on H.R. 3808," Judiciary.house.gov, March 7, 2012.

I sincerely sympathize with [the] family [of Dennis McCann, who was killed by an undocumented drunk driver in 2011]. The criminal justice system failed this family and allowed a tragedy to occur. The perpetrator in that circumstance, an individual with a significant criminal history, should not have been released from custody. Not for reasons associated with his immigration status however, but for his demonstrated behavior and the threat his actions posed to public safety. H.R. 3808 [which would require the deportation of undocumented immigrants arrested for drunk driving] will not resolve situations such as this. I believe, in fact, it has the potential to increase the likelihood of a similar catastrophe occurring to another family.

As set forth in H.R. 3808, the loose interpretation of the reasonable standard pertaining to immigration status checks will undoubtedly place more individuals into the criminal justice system awaiting determination. In essence, this proposed legislation will create a de-facto mandatory detention program. Compulsory incarceration, especially of status, misdemeanor or traffic offenders, dramatically increases stress on an already overcrowded detention system, necessitating the release of criminal offenders back into our neighborhoods. For example, the Salt Lake County [Utah] Jail currently [in 2012] releases between 700 and 900 criminals monthly for reasons of overcrowding. Last year, the Salt Lake City Police Department booked an individual for exposing himself to children on an elementary school playground. That individual spent 45 minutes in jail prior to being released due to overcrowding. We are fortunate this particular individual was not predisposed to engage in more serious criminal activity following his release, such as actually abducting or injuring a child.

Profiling Is Ineffective and Risky

It is vital that legislation and laws target and address the root problem, not ancillary circumstances of a specific isolated situation. February 2007, in Salt Lake City, an 18 year-old Bosnian refugee went on a violent rampage in a local shopping mall,

Police investigate the victim of a mass shooting by a Bosnian immigrant in Salt Lake City, Utah, in 2007. The author cites this as an example of focusing on a criminal's immigrant status rather than on the crime itself, which is what proposed laws targeting immigrant drunk drivers do, he says.

killing five and injuring several others before responding officers took his life. Immediate sentiment from the community would have undoubtedly supported the rounding up of all Bosnian immigrants in our city and detaining them for questioning. As overreaching and ridiculous as this seems, is this bill not moving us in the same direction? The young man in our mall situation was not motivated by religious belief, ethnicity, or even violent video games. He was simply an individual who found the wrong outlet for his personal circumstance. As the fight against terrorism has demonstrated extensively, profiling on the basis of appearance is ineffective and in fact exposes us to greater risk, allowing individuals exhibiting behavioral indicators to go unnoticed.

I would be proud, as would my colleagues, to be involved in the drafting of effective legislation that addresses all repeat offenders of DUI [driving under the influence] laws and works to prevent this crime from reoccurring. DUI is a preventable crime, it is not a crime of passion, but an act of irresponsibility. Many of our drivers do not recognize the impact of their actions or understand the level of impairment that accompanies alcohol consumption. Across the nation, states have refused to publish driver rules and regulations in languages other than English. As a nation proud of its immigrant heritage, this seems shortsighted. Is not an educated motoring public important?

A Statistically Insignificant Issue

It is estimated there are more than 11 million undocumented individuals residing in the United States. Studies conducted by the Rand Institute and the Consortium for Police Leadership in Equity found that undocumented individuals actually under-commit crimes compared to other segments of the population. There is certainly no indication they drive intoxicated at a higher rate. Why then should we draft legislation that does not focus on the significant problem of driving while intoxicated in our nation, but focuses on a statistically insignificant issue. Please understand that for the McCann family, this most certainly is in no way insignificant or minor. It is incumbent upon lawmakers and those who enforce the laws to maintain an unemotional evaluation of what is correct and proper when drafting and applying laws that govern our great nation.

H.R. 3808 invites racial profiling by requiring state and local law enforcement officers to check federal databases based on "reasonable ground to believe the person is an alien." The invitation or quite frankly the encouragement to racially profile or to interject bias is exacerbated by the bill's use of the over-broad term "apprehended" rather than convicted, which at least implies due process. The phrase facilitates pre-textual checking or verification of immigration status. In this way, H.R. 3808 is a national version of Arizona's controversial S.B. [Senate Bill] 1070 and Alabama's H.B. [House Bill] 56. Both of which invite racial profiling by requiring officers to determine immigration status based on reasonable suspicion that a person is unlawfully present. Due to concerns regarding federal preemption, the Department of Justice has filed suit in both these states, as well as the state of Utah, to block this type of detrimental and misguided legislation.

Inappropriate Delegation of Authority

This bill authorizes state and local officers to issue detainers for any and all apprehended immigrants, thereby inappropriately delegating authority to such officers, absent training and accountability. We have seen the failure first hand of immigration programs, such as the 287(g) program which co-ops local law enforcement as immigration agents without oversight. Atrocious law enforcement abuses occurring both within the program and outside have led the Department of Justice to conduct investigations and issue indictments in Maricopa County, Arizona, as well as East Haven, Connecticut. At least under a flawed 287(g) agreement, the involved officers received training. The Administration has drastically reduced funding to the program and has indicated it will not enter into any new agreements. H.R. 3808 sidesteps any official agreement or training, exposing officers, agencies and the public to abuses and complaints, thereby degrading public cooperation and trust.

The expansion of mandatory detention to any undocumented person who is apprehended but not convicted for a misdemeanor offense ties the hands of the law enforcement system and will result in costly, unnecessary and potentially lengthy detentions. Immigration and Customs Enforcement already has ample authority to detain and make detention decisions based upon the factors of risk to the public and risk of flight. In fact, ICE's [US Immigration and Customs Enforcement] guidance for trial attorneys identifies DUI as a high priority.

A Federal Responsibility

This bill inappropriately sets local law enforcement priorities. Perspective is imperative when allocating the limited and ever-shrinking resources of law enforcement agencies throughout the

The Myth of Criminality Among Immigrants

There is no relationship between violent crime and the immigrant share of a population.

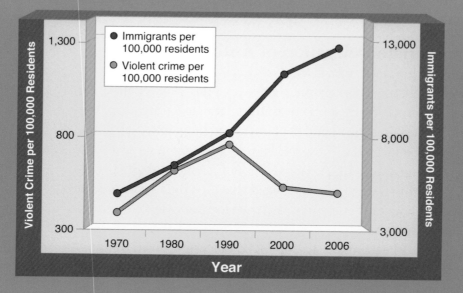

Taken from: Steven A. Camarota and Jessica Vaughan. "Immigration and Crime: Assessing a Conflicted Issue." Center for Immigration Studies, November 2009. www.cis.org.

country. Our cities face drive-by shootings, homicides, sexual assaults, and ever increasing dangers from prescription drug diversion. Not to diminish the impact of driving while intoxicated, should the federal government set that as a priority in our cities above all others? Currently [in 2012], mandatory arrest is connected almost exclusively to instances of domestic violence and no other criminal activity. In the state of Utah, DUI is a misdemeanor traffic offense. Typically, officers process suspected individuals in the station, constituting a breath alcohol content analysis and issuing a citation for first time offenses. The process takes between 30 minutes to an hour. If now officers are required to transport individuals to jail due to mandatory DUI protocol or immigration status checks, the typical out of service time becomes two hours. That is two hours that an officer is not on the street stopping other DUI drivers or criminal perpetrators. Immigration status now becomes the priority, not criminal behavior.

Major Cities Chiefs, a professional association of Chiefs and Sheriffs representing the 69 largest cities in the United States and Canada, recently reiterated its position on immigration. This document emphasizes the commitment of member agencies to enforce criminal violations of law regardless of citizenship status; however, the group is unanimous in its position that immigration enforcement is a federal responsibility. Placing local law enforcement officers in the position of immigration agents undermines the trust and cooperation essential to successful community-oriented policing. We do not possess adequate resources or training to appropriately undertake such a federal mandate and, in fact, believe it significantly detracts from the core mission of local police to create safe communities.

Reasonable Policing Requires Reasonable Legislation

In order to be successful in our mission, local law enforcement must have the cooperation of all members of our communities. In Salt Lake City, approximately one third of the population is Latino and subject to inappropriate, or disproportionate, police scrutiny under H.R. 3808. Often unrecognized in the immigration debate is the efficacy of enforcement and the adverse impact upon all individuals of color. How is a police officer to determine "that the individual is an alien unlawfully present in the United States" without detaining and questioning anyone who speaks, looks or acts as if they might be from another nation? Is it not racial bias to subject certain individuals—based solely on a surname or skin color—to a different standard or practice than others with whom we interact?

On its face, this bill appears unconstitutional, as it violates the anti-commandeering doctrine in Justice [Antonin] Scalia's majority opinion in *Printz v. U.S.* [which ruled unconstitutional certain provisions of the Brady Act, the 1993 law that put into effect federal background checks on those purchasing firearms]. That doctrine generally prevents federal law from establishing blanket requirements for state and local officers. Federal law can incentivize state and local conduct through grants, but it cannot simply require certain actions. The type of background checks identified and required in this bill are directly parallel to those required by Congress in the interim rules of the Brady Act, that the Court declared unconstitutional.

I am extremely proud to be a law enforcement officer and am represented by many fine individuals, not only in my own agency but throughout the nation. The standard by which we judge successful police interaction is reasonableness. We expect our officers to interact in a responsible and prudent manner with every member of the public, including those who have engaged in criminal activity. In order to provide these outstanding men and women with the support they deserve, it is incumbent upon us, as policy and lawmakers, to ensure we provide them reasonable legislation.

SEVEN

Sobriety Checkpoints Are Effective in Preventing Drunk Driving

Texas Transportation Institute

The Texas Transportation Institute is a research agency affiliated with the Texas A&M University System that focuses on solving transportation problems. In this viewpoint the author explains how sobriety checkpoints work and gives an overview of evidence supporting their effectiveness in reducing alcohol-related accidents. The author responds to criticisms of sobriety checkpoints based on their low arrest rates and says that such rates are not a suitable measure of the effectiveness of checkpoints, which work by deterring potential drunk drivers through the threat of arrest. According to formal and informal polls, it is also clear that there is support for the use of sobriety checkpoints both from the general public and from those working in the justice system.

A sobriety checkpoint is a roadblock set up by law enforcement officers to detect and deter impaired driving in locations where there is a high incidence of crashes and fatalities. At checkpoints, multiple law enforcement officers (ranging in number from 2 to 15 or more) funnel all traffic into a controlled area and perform brief interviews (10–30 seconds) with drivers to determine if they are impaired by alcohol or other substances. If the interviewing officer suspects impairment, the officer directs the driver out of the flow of traffic to a secondary officer for further impairment screening.

Overview of Research Results

- The Centers for Disease Control [and Prevention] (CDC) recommends sobriety checkpoints as an effective countermeasure for motor-vehicle injury prevention based on strong evidence presented in peer-reviewed research.
- An overview of the research from the past 30 years [since the 1980s] consistently demonstrates that sobriety checkpoints reduce alcohol-impaired crashes by 20% and fatal crashes thought to involve alcohol by 20% and 26%.
- Officers make one arrest every 6.5 hours when using checkpoints, compared to one arrest every 7.5 hours on regular patrol.
- Checkpoint Tennessee, one of the most frequently cited, methodologically sound, and rigorous studies, found a 20.4% reduction of alcohol-related fatalities. The deterrent effect lasted for almost two years following the conclusion of the checkpoint program.
- Sobriety checkpoints have a strong return on investment: $144 to $1.
- Sobriety checkpoints can be successfully operated with just a few officers.
- Although surveys did not specifically focus on Texas, national and targeted opinion polls found strong support for the use of sobriety checkpoints (73%) even among those who reported that they have driven after drinking during the last month (57%).
- Thirty-eight states conduct sobriety checkpoints, some more frequently than others—those that do not conduct sobriety checkpoints either consider them illegal by law or state constitution or the state provides no explicit authority to conduct them or prohibits them based on their interpretation of the U.S. Constitution (as of 2/2011).

Effectiveness and Efficiency of Sobriety Checkpoints

Critics frequently point to the low arrest rate at sobriety checkpoints to argue they are unsuccessful. This criticism represents a fundamental misunderstanding of how checkpoints work. Checkpoints measure success differently than traditional law enforcement techniques, which focus on the number of arrests. A successful sobriety checkpoint program increases the real or perceived risk of being arrested for driving while intoxicated. If a driver is deciding between driving while intoxicated or designating a driver, they will likely consider the risk of arrest and the resulting punishment from choosing to drive. A successful checkpoint program increases the risk of arrest (real or perceived), and influences a motorist to choose to not drive while intoxicated. As a result of this deterrent effect, checkpoints regularly decrease impaired crashes by 15%–20%.

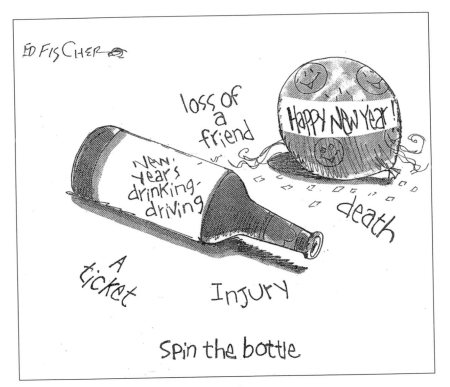

"Spin the Bottle," by Ed Fischer. www.Cartoonstock.com.

However, if one considers an alternative measure for arrest rates—the number of hours between arrests per officer, sobriety checkpoints can have higher arrest rates than standard enforcement practices. One study found that "officers make one arrest every 6.5 hours when using checkpoints, compared to one arrest every 7.5 hours on regular patrol." Additionally, time spent by officers interviewing unimpaired drivers is not wasted; these interactions provide the impetus for the community to recognize an increased arrest risk when driving while intoxicated, and respond by choosing not to engage in this activity. A more accurate and

A police officer arrests a woman after she fails a sobriety test at a checkpoint. Checkpoints are roadblocks set up by law enforcement to detect and deter impaired drivers.

frequently used measure of a successful checkpoint is the amount of crime deterred, not solely the number of drivers arrested.

In the Checkpoint Tennessee study, one of the most frequently cited, methodologically sound, and rigorous studies, researchers found that the program reduced alcohol impaired driving facilities by 20.4%. The program placed 12 checkpoints across the state every weekend for 12 months—from March 1994 to March 1995. On five different weekends, local police used a blitz scheme where officers implemented small checkpoints in each of the state's 95 counties. The program included a statewide media campaign to raise awareness of the checkpoint program, including a television spot, a billboard campaign and press releases. Extensive news coverage from local television stations, newspapers and radio stations supplemented the media campaign.

Proven Benefits and Public Support

The researchers evaluating the Checkpoint Tennessee project developed a model to measure alcohol-related fatal crashes for Tennessee and each of its surrounding states. This approach was taken to ensure that any measurable changes were attributable to the checkpoint program and not a result of a larger, regional change. The model showed a reduction of approximately nine alcohol-related fatal crashes per month (or a 20.4% reduction). The model found a statistically insignificant increase in fatalities for the surrounding states. The total cost of the program was $927,594, with approximately half of the funds paid by a federal government grant, and half paid by the state. According to the National Highway Traffic Safety Administration (NHTSA) estimate of $977,000 in costs per alcohol-related fatality, for every dollar invested by Tennessee and the federal government, $114 was returned in cost savings from averted fatalities.

The American Automobile Association Foundation for Traffic Safety (AAA Foundation) annually conducts national polls on various traffic safety questions. In 2009, the poll found that 72.8% of Americans support the use of sobriety checkpoints in their community multiple times per month. Only 8.9% of respondents did not support the use of sobriety checkpoints. Even a majority (57%) of drivers who self-reported driving after drinking in the past month supported sobriety checkpoints.

Support from Stakeholders

In general, the feedback from prosecution and judicial representatives contacted during the development of this research summary supported the idea of allowing sobriety checkpoints as an impaired driving countermeasure. The stakeholders agreed that the State should not prohibit law enforcement from using a tool that has been found to be effective in multiple environments to reduce crashes and alter driving after drinking behavior.

Issues were raised regarding [the] potential challenges by the defense, but the issue of probable cause is also part of traditional traffic stops that are based on driving behavior. The stakeholders recognize that the major focus of sobriety checkpoints is the deterrence effect of drivers choosing not to drive after drinking.

It should be noted that if sobriety checkpoints are deemed acceptable by statute, law enforcement, and, subsequently, corresponding jurisdictional communities, will make a conscious choice about whether to employ them as an impaired-driving countermeasure. Sobriety checkpoints are only one tool, albeit an effective tool, that law enforcement and their associated communities can utilize to address alcohol-impaired-driving problems in local areas. Saturation and targeted patrols conducted by DWI [driving while intoxicated] or traffic units within local law enforcement agencies, as well as general patrol officers, will continue to operate in addition to any use of sobriety checkpoints.

EIGHT

Sobriety Checkpoints Are Ineffective in Preventing Drunk Driving

Patrick Adams

> Patrick Adams is a libertarian activist whose work focuses on eliminating the use of police checkpoints. In the viewpoint below he questions the constitutionality of these checkpoints, particularly sobriety checkpoints. He says that not only do these checkpoints violate a citizen's Fourth Amendment rights, there is also abundant evidence that they are ineffective in stopping drunk driving. Adams compares sobriety checkpoints to saturation patrols, in which a large number of police officers patrol a specific area known to have a high volume of drunk drivers, looking for behaviors indicating impaired driving. Saturation patrols are shown to be more effective and use far less resources than sobriety checkpoints, he says. Furthermore, saturation patrols only require drivers to prove that they are driving sober once the police have seen evidence that they may not be, while sobriety checkpoints treat all drivers as guilty until proved innocent.

Imagine driving to the local school to pick up your kids. It's three o'clock in the afternoon, and the day is unseasonably nice. The sun is shining and your otherwise routine schedule is pleasant enough. You drive around a final corner to reach your destination when you suddenly approach a group of police cars. You abruptly halt and observe several officers standing right in the middle of the street. They signal you to stop. You pull up to the stopping point and roll down your window, wondering what could be happening.

The first officer announces that you have encountered a police checkpoint. He asks to see your driver license, registration, and insurance card. You present these items and ask if there is anything wrong. "Just a routine checkpoint," is the casual reply. He sizes up your papers and asks, "Are you the owner of the vehicle?" You reply affirmatively. He then scours your vehicle, both inside and out. The officer focuses on your youngest child in her car seat. He pokes his head about the back window opening, further examining the seat. He states nonchalantly, "Just checking for proper restraints on everyone in the car, ma'am." Your papers are handed back to you with a detached thank you. The officer signals you to proceed. "Have a nice day, ma'am."

This scenario is an all too common occurrence in America. A checkpoint, or roadblock as it is sometimes called, is a police technique that seeks to enforce various laws by stopping and engaging motorists without suspicion. The most familiar type of checkpoint might be those based on sobriety, but many other types exist. There are checkpoints for driver license, registration, insurance, seatbelts, child seats, safety inspections, citizenship, hunting, boating, and even fireworks. Judicially documented cases of sobriety checkpoints began to appear in the early to mid-1980s. Other checkpoints can be judicially traced back to the mid-1970s.

Perceived Expedience

The legality of checkpoints varies by state. The Insurance Institute for Highway Safety notes that sobriety checkpoints are illegal in 11 states; however, various other types of checkpoints have occurred in most, if not all, of these 11 states. The 1990 *Michigan State Police v. Sitz* Supreme Court decision ruled that sobriety checkpoints are basically constitutional, and generally left it up to each state to determine that application.

Checkpoints are widespread, so the pointed question for the libertarian is how checkpoints can be so omnipresent in the face of clearly violating the spirit of the fourth amendment. The answer might actually have nothing to do with the fourth amendment, but rather everything to do with perceived expedience. It was Chief Justice William Rehnquist who shamefully dismissed the fourth amendment in his majority *Sitz* opinion. Rehnquist favored expedience when he declared that checkpoint effectiveness determination ". . . remains with the governmental officials who have a unique understanding of, and a responsibility for, limited public resources, including a finite number of police officers." A dissenting Justice [John Paul] Stevens (joined by Justice [Thurgood] Marshall and Justice [William] Brennan) correctly deferred to the fourth amendment, but still entertained the expedience approach of Rehnquist. That approach was dubious, at best, with testimony from sheriffs and other officers confirming that approaches to drunk driving which did not use checkpoints simply worked better.

Flawed Research

The evidence regarding checkpoint effectiveness fared no better in the scientific and scholarly literature. The Centers for Disease Control [and Prevention (CDC)] review of 23 studies from the 1980s and 1990s touted checkpoint success, but a closer look revealed flawed execution and spurious relationships. The CDC rated the studies' methodologies, ranking only three as "good." The other 20 were rated "fair."

A closer examination of the Centers for Disease Control [and Prevention] studies revealed the details of those problems; problems cited by CDC itself. CDC suggested that results from the 1997 Voas study [conducted by Robert Voas, a prominent researcher on alcohol and highway safety,] ". . . are confounded due to overlap in media markets across intervention and comparison communities and checkpoint activities in comparison communities. A zero tolerance law for young drivers was implemented in California during the intervention period." The conclusion of another study was "Well publicized roving patrols produced similar effects to checkpoints." The 1990 [David] Levy study had "Serious problems with colinearity with publicity campaigns in model." Over half of the studies cited evidence from countries that perform random breath testing for motorists, an experience relatively unknown in the U.S. Scientists and others might even theorize about other confounding variables that possibly made an impact in the overall anti-drunk driving campaign aggressively implemented at the beginning of the 1980s.

Checkpoint Ineffectiveness

The evidence for checkpoint ineffectiveness continued into the 2000s. The FBI weighed in when it compared saturation patrols [involving a large number of police officers in a designated area looking for drivers who appear to be impaired] to checkpoints in Ohio, Missouri, and Tennessee. The comparison showed that "Overall, measured in arrests per hour, a dedicated saturation patrol is the most effective method of apprehending offenders." That sentiment was echoed later in the year [2003] by the journal *Accident Analysis and Prevention* in its survey of law enforcement. It stated that "States with infrequent checkpoints claimed a lack of funding and police resources for not conducting more checkpoints, preferred saturation patrols over checkpoints because they were more 'productive,' and used large numbers of police officers at checkpoints."

Newspapers picked up on these findings, and their investigations confirmed the literature. A *Hagerstown Herald-Mail* interview of Maryland State Police Commander David Kloos revealed the squandered resource management and limited return on checkpoint operations. Kloos confirmed that a saturation patrol costs a fraction of a checkpoint and actually yields more arrests. The paltry arrest rates in Maryland's checkpoint programs a generation earlier might make one question why a failed program persisted.

No Deterrent Effect Found

If checkpoints do not result in arrests, then motorists might wonder about their purpose. Checkpoint supporters suggest deterrence as a purpose, but again, the evidence does not support the claim. The Maryland anti-drunk driving campaign called Checkpoint Strikeforce was evaluated for deterrence. The review found that there was no deterrent effect, whether for public perceptions, driving behaviors, or alcohol-related motor vehicle crashes and injuries. If one is not convinced by that study, would it not be logical to conclude that publicity regarding saturation patrols could just as easily be done as publicity for checkpoints? A press release by the Las Vegas Police Department last New Year's Eve [2011] emphasized police presence. "If you're driving impaired, look for the police behind you, because that's where we're going to be,"

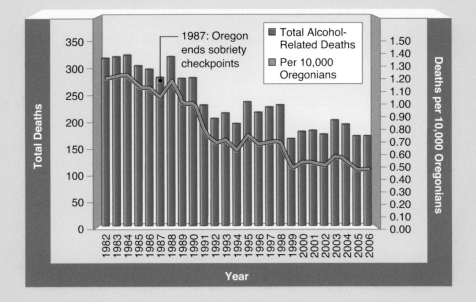

Alcohol–Related Deaths Continued Falling Even After Oregon Ended Checkpoints

Taken from: Karl Chisolm. "No, Sobriety Checkpoints Don't Save Lives." Blue Oregon, April 1, 2009. www.blueoregon.com.

says Captain Mark Tavarez. "It doesn't matter where you are in town." That sentiment was echoed by Lieutenant Adrian Vasquez of the Colorado Springs [Colorado] Police Department, a municipality that eliminated checkpoints in 2011. Vasquez explained regarding saturation patrols that "We've come to a realization that we actually get more bang for the buck from high visibility enforcements."

Other issues of concern to law enforcement include legal loopholes and new technologies (e.g., texting) that allow drivers to immediately alert others regarding checkpoint locations. Various officers have voiced these concerns, in addition to the dominant argument of saturation patrols. Some of these concerns have resulted in positive action, including the Costa Mesa, California police chief announcing his plans to eliminate checkpoints. The aforementioned police department in Colorado Springs and sheriff of that county also announced abandonment of checkpoints; however, it remains to be seen if the state police will implement their own roadblocks.

Not Practical or Principled

Courts have apparently dropped the ball on checkpoints, shelving the fourth amendment for perceived expedience. Some in law enforcement are willing to state the truth about checkpoints, but persistence of the method is still too widespread. That seemingly leaves state legislatures to address the issue. Utah and New Hampshire recently introduced bills that would limit the types of checkpoints discussed in this article. Legislation to implement checkpoints in Washington, Oregon, and Texas failed in 2011. The Oregon legislation actually proposed carving out an exception to the search and seizure clause of that state's constitution. It is fortunate that all three of these state efforts failed fairly early in the process. The proposed legislation in Texas failed for an eighth straight year. A similar, current proposal in Wisconsin is likely to fail because no action has been taken on it since last year [2011].

This article has, thus far, focused on the practical aspects of checkpoints. The libertarian, however, might fairly inquire about aspects of principle. Some libertarians will even find it galling to concede principle in favor of practicalities (I actually had this conversation with two men who had unpleasant checkpoint experiences). The libertarian might ask, "What if checkpoints *are* shown to be effective?" The historical answer to that question has always been negative. Checkpoint design virtually guarantees ineffectiveness in the future. Effectiveness is precluded by the simple concept of passivity. That passivity is law enforcement contained in one spot, waiting for something to happen. Police wait for lawbreakers to approach them, while interacting with the law-abiding. The classic *guilty until proven innocent* is unequivocally contrary to the concept and practicality embodied in the fourth amendment.

Guilty Until Proven Innocent?

It is heartening to know that some have not forsaken principle. Justice Brennan wrote in *Sitz* that ". . . consensus that a particular law enforcement technique serves a laudable purpose has never been the touchstone of constitutional analysis." Justice Stevens recognized the unbridled discretion that officers could exercise at a checkpoint, discretion perhaps far different from that outlined in a policy manual or PR [public relations] campaign. He stated, "A Michigan officer who questions a motorist at a sobriety checkpoint has virtually unlimited discretion to detain the driver on the basis of the slightest suspicion. . . . Any driver who had just consumed a glass of beer, or even a sip of wine, would almost certainly have the burden of demonstrating to the officer that her driving ability was not impaired." It is this type of scenario that led MADD founder Candace Lightner to denounce the organization she founded. Lightner stated, "[MADD has] become far more neoprohibitionist than I had ever wanted or envisioned. . . . I didn't start MADD to deal with alcohol. I started MADD to deal with the issue of drunk driving." The American Beverage Institute also asserts that the dinner wine sip has become problematic. Justice Stevens conjured up memories of those late night movies of Nazis requesting "Papers, please," when he declared that

Critics of sobriety checkpoints say they treat all drivers as guilty until proven innocent—just the opposite of what the law is supposed to do.

". . . unannounced investigatory seizures are . . . the hallmark of regimes far different from ours."

The admonitions of these dissenting justices were not, unfortunately, enough to carry the day in *Sitz*. Their arguments however, provide an excellent foundation on which to approach this issue. We know that *guilty until proven innocent* is irreconcilable with the fourth amendment. Checkpoint supporters however, are unable, or willing, to make that connection. Their erroneous, perceived expedience is a glaring logical, and arguably moral, failure. Checkpoint supporters, in short, are not interested in your liberties. I propose that their practical reasons are so statistically wrong as to make them readily vulnerable in their arguments. You can, in short, keep the constitutional principle close at hand, while still overcoming erroneous claims of checkpoint success.

If that task seems difficult in our current day, then I would point to evidence of hope referred to in this article: defeated checkpoint legislation, proposed anti-checkpoint legislation, law enforcement abandoning checkpoints, and the other voices cautioning us about what works and what does not work.

Evidence of Hope

Legislation is our hope. I believe the Utah State Senate was afraid to debate the recent checkpoint bill simply because they did not have a reasoned argument. I think the bill will resurface in the near future. If so, then hopefully Utahans will be even more diligent in making their voices heard. This can be done with simple technology, such as sending an email to a representative or senator. Elected officials often listen to these correspondences, especially those that are thoughtful and compelling.

Education is our hope. Technology has vastly contributed to the understanding of issues that we care about. Discussion groups, YouTube videos, and alternative newscasts are an excellent way to have a dialogue about issues important to liberty. Those issues might not get covered by the 6 o'clock news, but you can bet many concerned people are discussing them on the internet.

Participation is our hope. The technology of the internet brought out these issues, but it is time to push these issues to the next level. Conversations with local lawmakers and executive branch officials (e.g., mayors) have been made easier with technology. Emails are a simple way to voice your concerns and even keep in touch. Local government meetings are often sparsely attended, so what better way to get your politician's ear than by becoming part of a meeting's agenda? Open records requests also means knowing what is happening (and not happening) at checkpoints. The reports of local police regarding each checkpoint are public information through the Freedom of Information Act.

Preserving Our Rights

Participation can be even more effective when one does not participate. Know your rights at a checkpoint. You cannot be compelled to incriminate yourself. Distinctions and guidelines for various types of checkpoints (e.g., sobriety vs. driver license) have been lost in what often sounds like a morass of legal double-talk, but a basic familiarity with law enforcement restrictions can still go a long way in preserving your rights. An audio or video device will also help in recording encounters, especially to protect yourself. This is not to suggest that you will be seeking conflict, but simply to have a record of any police indiscretion that might occur.

Is the tide turning regarding support for checkpoints? Some evidence seems to suggest that support is eroding for checkpoints, so I am cautiously optimistic. My hope is that legislation, education, and participation will contribute to reclaiming one slice of the fourth amendment.

NINE

Ignition Interlock Devices Should Be Required of All Convicted Drunk Drivers

Rebecca Kanable

In the following viewpoint Rebecca Kanable, a writer with a focus on law enforcement issues, asserts the effectiveness of ignition interlock devices, which prevent vehicles from starting if the driver's blood alcohol concentration level is above the legal limit. In municipalities where these devices are used, they are generally installed in the vehicles of drivers with at least one drunk driving conviction as a means of preventing subsequent offenses. In addition to decreasing alcohol-related accidents, Kanable says, these devices also cost local governments much less than alcohol-related accidents do, because the offenders themselves bear the cost. Nevertheless, Kanable laments, only ten states currently require all offenders to use ignition interlock devices.

Ignition interlocks are a vehicle sanction. They prevent people from driving drunk, breaking the law, damaging property and causing injury or death. If a driver's blood alcohol concentration is above a pre-set number, a vehicle won't start.

Rebecca Kanable, "Advancing Ignition Interlocks," *Law Enforcement Technology*, vol. 37, no. 8, August 2010. Copyright © 2010 by Law Enforcement Technology. All rights reserved. Reproduced by permission.

Describing ignition interlocks metaphorically, they are a 24/7 probation officer in the front seat of an offender's vehicle. Those are the words of Richard Roth, Ph.D. and retired physics professor and citizen lobbyist for effective, cost-effective and fair DUI [driving under the influence] laws since 1998.

Numerous studies have proven ignition interlocks are one of the most effective ways to prevent drunk driving.

Interlock technology increasingly offers more advantages from GPS [Global Positioning System], data recording, photo imaging and instant reporting to probation officers. The number of mandatory programs is also increasing. In 2009, about 180,000 interlocks were installed into vehicles. In his "2009 Annual Survey of Currently Installed Ignition Interlocks in the United States," Roth calculates that's a 23 percent increase over 2008.

Yet, he says that number represents only about 13 percent of those arrested for drunk driving, or about 15 interlocks per alcohol-impaired driving fatality.

Though the use of ignition interlocks is not mandated as widely as some proponents would like, efforts are underway to move ignition interlocks forward.

Interlock Proponents

Robert Voas has been studying alcohol and highway safety for 40 years and saw the first interlock in 1970. Initially as director of the National Highway Traffic Safety Administration's (NHTSA's) Office of Program Evaluation, and more recently as principal investigator for government research programs in drunk driving and community alcohol problem prevention, Voas holds a Ph.D. in psychology and is a senior research scientist at the Pacific Institute for Research and Evaluation (PIRE).

His research has found interlocks are currently one of the most effective methods for controlling the recidivism of drivers. When an interlock is installed in an offender's vehicle, he says it generally reduces recidivism by 65 percent.

Jail would be more effective, he adds, but is costly and not something that could be done for any lengthy period.

Toyota unveils its new ignition interlock device in 2009. These devices monitor blood alcohol concentration levels of drivers, which if too high, disable the vehicle's ignition.

Mothers Against Drunk Driving (MADD) supports legislation making interlocks mandatory for all convicted drunk drivers.

"The simple reason that drunk drivers continue to drink and drive is because they can," Laura Dean-Mooney, MADD national president, states testifying before the Senate Environment & Public Works Committee in April [2010].

Studies overwhelmingly show that interlocks work, she says. The Centers for Disease Control and Prevention (CDC) has reviewed ignition interlocks and stated that "Based on strong evidence of the effectiveness of interlocks in reducing re-arrest rates, the (CDC) Task Force recommended that ignition interlock programs be implemented."

In addition to the CDC, she points out there are more than 15 published studies on interlock effectiveness (involving diverse populations) that show interlocks are associated with substantial reductions in recidivism, ranging from 50 to 90 percent.

Cost-Effectiveness

Drunk driving has high costs for society.

Every day, 32 people in the United States die in motor vehicle crashes that involve an alcohol-impaired driver, according to NHTSA. The annual cost of alcohol-related vehicle crashes is more than $51 billion, according to a 2000 study funded by NHTSA.

Law enforcement knows first-hand the damage caused by drug driving. Each year there are more than 1.4 million DUI arrests (according to the FBI in 2003).

Paul Marques, who holds a Ph.D. in drug dependence research and is also a senior research scientist at PIRE, says the interlock is a good compromise between trying to control someone who threatens public safety and not controlling the person in such a strong way that the person cannot hold a job.

Offenders bear the costs of interlocks by paying a nominal administrative fee plus the costs of installing and maintaining an interlock device. Installation costs are about $150, and maintenance costs range from $60 to $80 per month, Roth says. A study by Marques found that with every dollar spent on interlocks for those with one DUI conviction, the public saves $3.

What's the Problem?

If interlocks are effective and cost-effective, why is it that only 10 states require all DUI offenders to use an ignition interlock device and two states highly incentivize DUI offenders to use an interlock. (In addition, California passed a pilot program requiring all convicted DUI offenders in four counties to use an ignition interlock device.)

Philip Cook, senior associate dean for faculty at Duke University, and Maeve Gearing, a doctoral student in public policy at Duke University, address this in "The Breathalyzer Behind the Wheel," a 2009 op-ed in *The New York Times*:

- Judges often fail to order installation, even when the law requires it. (Excuses include that offenders cannot afford them.)
- Offenders routinely ignore them.
- In areas where the installation is voluntary, few offenders choose [to] install them.

Furthermore, states have varying interlock laws. A proposed federal ignition interlock bill, if signed into law, will spur state governments to move quicker with ignition interlock mandates. If enacted, the Drunk Driving Repeat Offender Prevention Act of 2009 (DDROP) [reintroduced in 2011 and not yet in committee by January 2013] would withhold federal transportation funding from states that do not pass laws requiring at least six-month installations of ignition interlock devices in the private cars of all drivers convicted of drunk driving.

Technology Down the Road

Looking at the technology, Voas says there's interest in being able to positively identify the driver so a rolling retest [a retest done after beginning to drive] may not be necessary. One approach to this has been photo imaging. Voas predicts that a system that can take pictures of an offender as he's blowing into the interlock mouthpiece will increase in popularity. Currently [in 2010] two companies offer this technology.

One of those companies also has adapted a device from its interlock system to monitor drinking overall, not only drinking and driving. The portable breath tester has a timing unit that requires a breath test at court-specified intervals to ensure an offender is not drinking.

"This gives us an alternative method of monitoring and controlling drinking drivers who don't have cars into which they can install an interlock," Voas says.

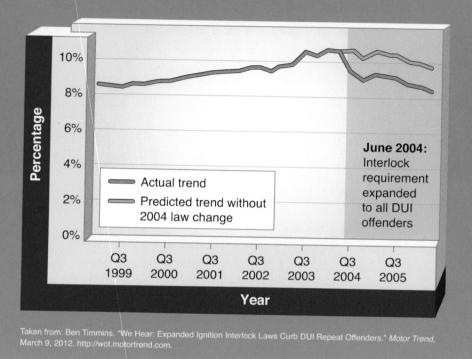

Expanded Ignition Interlock Laws Curb DUI Repeat Offenders

Percentage vs. Year

- Actual trend
- Predicted trend without 2004 law change

June 2004: Interlock requirement expanded to all DUI offenders

Taken from: Ben Timmins. "We Hear: Expanded Ignition Interlock Laws Curb DUI Repeat Offenders." *Motor Trend*, March 9, 2012. http://wot.motortrend.com.

One system under development to prevent drinking and driving is a passive, or transparent, system that would go into every new car. Only if that passive system detected alcohol in the car, would the driver be tested for alcohol. That might involve a breath test or an infrared system that could determine BAC [blood alcohol concentration] through the skin.

While work on a new system is underway, Voas suspects it is at least a decade before such a system becomes reality.

Changing Behavior Long Term

A benefit of interlocks is they control people temporarily and create a record of data.

"If a government has the resources, they could use the interlock data to monitor a person more actively: they could insist on treatment concurrent with the interlock, they could measure alcohol biomarkers from the blood or urine samples," Marques says.

"Overall, they could target in on the level of drinking of [an] individual and make hard recommendations for how that person must change in order to no longer endanger public safety."

The number of people who die as a result of alcohol-impaired driving crashes has remained relatively flat during the last 15 years or so [since the mid-1990s], Marques points out. (According to NHTSA, an estimated 11,773 people died in alcohol-impaired driving crashes in 2008.)

A common objection to installing interlocks is they don't need to be installed on the vehicles of first offenders. Marques says that corresponds with the popular myth that the first offender is someone who drove drunk only once and got caught.

The reality is someone arrested for drunken driving has driven impaired many times. Studies indicate the average person convicted of DUI for the first time has driven drunk at least 87 times before being caught.

"With about two-thirds of all DUI offenders being first offenders, we need to start dealing with this largest group to make a significant impact on the problem," Marques says.

No More Catch and Release

The interlock, like sobriety checkpoints and passive alcohol sensors, is a tool to keep drunken drivers off the road.

For too long in America, Dean-Mooney says, "we have been practicing a 'catch and release' program: law enforcement does their very best to catch drunk drivers, and we as a society through our legislatures and courts, often times let them go with few consequences."

To realize a nation without drunken driving, she says, "we must substantially increase the use of ignition interlocks to include all convicted drunk driving offenders."

TEN

Ignition Interlock Devices Are Unreliable

David C. Pilato

> David C. Pilato, a former assistant district attorney in Westchester County, New York, currently practices criminal defense law in Rochester, New York. In this viewpoint Pilato addresses New York State's 2010 passage of Leandra's Law, which mandates the installation of ignition interlock devices (IIDs) for all driving while intoxicated convicts. According to Pilato, these devices have historically been known both to malfunction and to provide inaccurate results, which could lead to wrongful resentencing. They were originally designed to prevent someone from driving drunk, not to provide evidence in a sentence violation hearing, a purpose for which they prove too unreliable. An additional problem with the law's IID provision, Pilato says, is the lack of financial support it provides to municipalities that are charged with installing, maintaining, and monitoring the devices.

On Aug. 15 [2010], the final provisions of [New York State's] Leandra's Law mandating the installation and maintenance of an ignition interlock device [IID] as part of every DWI [driving while intoxicated] sentence became effective.

"Trials and Tribulations: Ignition Interlock: False Positives, Lack of Funding," *The Daily Record*, September 1, 2010. Copyright © 2012 Dolan Media Newswires. Written by David C. Pilato, Esq., associate with The Wolford Law Firm LLP in Rochester, N.Y.

Named in memory of 11-year-old Leandra Rosado, who was killed in a drunk-driving accident in October 2009, Leandra's Law is the November 2009 DWI legislation that amended the Vehicle and Traffic Law, Penal Law and Executive Law.

One of its provisions created a new class E felony for anyone who operates a motor vehicle under the influence of alcohol or drugs while a child who is 15 years old or younger is a passenger in the vehicle. Other than the amendments concerning IIDs, the law took effect Dec. 18, 2009, applicable only to crimes committed after the Nov. 18, 2009 enactment date and sentenced after Dec. 18, 2009.

While much attention has been given to the expectation of increased highway safety and reduced rates of DWI recidivism, the new provisions are not without controversy. Although their efficacy has been touted in recent years, IIDs have a history of inaccuracy and malfunction. Their evidentiary value in the event someone is alleged to have violated the terms of his or her sentence based on a positive IID reading should be questioned. A false positive reading from a device with an unreliable track record could lead to a wrongful resentence. The lack of state funding for the IID programs also adds to the controversy.

The new ignition interlock law requires anyone convicted of driving while intoxicated to install and maintain an IID in every car they own or operate. The ignition interlock provision mandates that the court's sentence "shall" include the use of an IID for at least six months. Even first-time misdemeanor offenders sentenced to a conditional discharge are subject to this penalty.

Designed for Prevention

An IID is a small device, like a Breathalyzer, installed in a motor vehicle, which estimates a person's blood alcohol content [BAC]. Before the motor vehicle can be started, the driver must first provide a breath sample. If the sample is greater than the programmed BAC (just a trace amount—0.025 percent), the mechanism prevents the engine from starting. Periodically, after the engine has been started, the IID will require additional breath samples—a rolling retest. The purpose is to prevent someone other than the driver from breathing into the device and allowing the intoxicated person to simply start the vehicle and drive.

If a sample is not provided, or the sample exceeds the pre-set BAC, the device will log the event, warn the driver, then start an alarm until the ignition is turned off or a clean sample is provided. The monitoring agency will be notified of all purported violations, and false positives could result in someone being charged with violating the terms of his or her sentence.

Designed as an order of protection in favor of society, and not simply as a sentence violation, it is a crime to run afoul of some specified IID requirements. [There are] criminal penalties for even an attempt to circumvent or tamper with an IID.

Although not a crime in and of itself, a sentence violation could be predicated based on a positive IID reading, either in an attempt to start a vehicle or during one of the rolling restarts. The act of blowing into an IID while operating a motor vehicle hardly is the controlled setting required for a DWI prosecution, therefore it should be questioned whether more should be required in order to resentence someone alleged to have violated a DWI sentence.

A History of False Positives

IIDs are known to provide false positive results. In a detailed hearing memorandum submitted in connection with a Massachusetts Registry Board of Appeal case, attorney Brian E. Simoneau, an expert on Massachusetts IID hearings, discussed three possible causes of a positive BAC reading—alcohol in the subject's breath sample; IID malfunction or another substance in the sample registering as ethanol (ethyl alcohol). Note that, in Massachusetts, an IID is mandatory after two operating under the influence convictions as a condition of driver's license reinstatement or Hardship License. A violation of the IID requirement could result in a license revocation from 10 years to life.

A May 2010 Fox News of Chicago report, "DUI Breath Interlock Devices Frequently Malfunction," found that false positive alcohol readings registered when the subject had not consumed any alcoholic beverages but had used mouthwash or ate pizza crust, Wonder Bread, hot dog buns and sourdough English muffins. . . .

Well known in the world of DWI defense, breath tests often measure chemicals with molecular structures similar to those found in alcohol, including white bread. Body chemistry also may lead to false positives. People with diabetes, acid reflux disease, or some cancers can show a positive alcohol reading on an IID when no alcohol was consumed. The temperature inside a vehicle and other environmental factors also can contribute to inaccurate results.

Questionable Accuracy and Reliability

Ignition interlock devices were designed as "lockout devices," not to function as evidentiary breath testing instruments. Their purpose was not to collect evidence that could be used at a sentence violation hearing, but rather to prevent someone from operating a vehicle at an intoxicated level. Their accuracy in testing one's actual BAC is far too questionable.

Given the inaccuracy of IIDs, it would be unfair to simply rely on their results without the prosecution laying the proper evidentiary foundation during the course of a violation of probation or conditional discharge hearing.

In *People v. Mertz* [1986], the Court of Appeals [of the State of New York] held that Breathalyzer results could be admitted in evidence when the prosecution first establishes that the machine is accurate, was working properly when the test was performed and that the test was properly administered. The decision notes that Breathalyzers' rate of accuracy in measuring blood alcohol content is recognized generally, and that tests are admissible if the prosecution has submitted evidence satisfying the latter two conditions.

Because of their lack of scientific reliability, IIDs are more akin to Alco-Sensor tests given at the scene by police officers in order to establish grounds for requesting an individual to submit to a Breathalyzer, and not additional reliable scientific evidence of intoxication.

The results of an Alco-Sensor test are inadmissible at trial to show intoxication.

Necessary Resources Not Provided

A second controversial aspect of the final Aug. 15 Leandra's Law provisions deals with the lack of funding with regard to implementing and monitoring IID programs. The law does not provide state funding for those who cannot afford the installation and rental fees. Similarly, it fails to provide money for the additional personnel required to monitor the program.

Persons convicted of DWI are responsible for the costs associated with the installation and maintenance of the devices. Generally the installation fee can cost as much as $125, in addition to rental fees of $69.50 to $100 per month, according to the state Office of Probation and Correctional Alternatives. For some, the fact that the IID will act as a scarlet letter in parking lots, garages and even on the open road is even more costly that the fees.

What is troubling some nearby counties is the fact that the IID program must be administered by the county—usually by county probation departments—not the state Department of Motor Vehicles. While it is likely counties are better equipped to handle the monitoring (already a probation department function), the counties argue that they simply do not have the necessary additional funding.

Resources are necessary to implement the program and train existing personnel, to hire and train new employees, and pay for overtime.

Good Intentions, Bad Implementation

Calling the changes an "unfunded mandate," Ontario County last month demanded the state [of New York] provide the necessary funding and suspended the probation department from overseeing IID monitoring until the state provides the funds. Wayne County, too, has shown resistance: At a July 9 [2010] county board meeting, Walworth [town] Supervisor Robert Plant initiated a resolu-

In 2010 New York governor David Paterson signs the Child Passenger Protection Act, or Leandra's Law. The law mandates the installation of ignition interlocking devices as part of every DWI sentence.

tion enabling the head of probation to ignore the state's direction to amend its monitoring plan.

Other [New York] counties also are pushing back against the law, including Fulton, Genesee, Schuyler, Steuben and Chemung. A June 13 [2010] article by James M. Wagman quoted Fulton

County Board of Supervisors Clerk Jon Stead, who said the law is on the right track but needs some tweaking: "I think what most of us are saying right now is the law was well intended but it's not being well implemented."

The same article quoted Fulton County Probation Director Mike Kirkpatrick: "Time is money . . . [a]nd that's where the unfunded mandate comes in. The state has made no provisions to date for the payment of this."

Messenger Post staff writer Mike Maslanik reported Aug. 30 [2010] that Ontario County's failure to comply with Albany's directives could lead to sanctions as well as exposure to potential lawsuits, according to Walt Cogswell, manager of Adult Operation at the state Division of Probation. Cogswell said that if someone is hurt or killed by a drunk driver who would have had an ignition interlock installed on the vehicle after a Leandra's Law conviction, the case could be made that the county was negligent through its failure to comply with state law.

Certainly the goals and the legislative intent that prompted Leandra's Law are shared by all—keep the roads safe and prevent senseless tragedies. Nevertheless, a history of unreliability and questionable evidentiary value make IIDs controversial.

ELEVEN

Lowering the Drinking Age Will Not Reduce Teen Alcohol Use and Abuse

Adrian Lund

> In the following viewpoint Adrian Lund, president of the Insurance Institute for Highway Safety and the Highway Data Loss Institute, responds to the campaign to lower the drinking age from twenty-one to eighteen in the United States. He argues that scientific data disprove this campaign's two main theses: that there are no proven benefits of raising the drinking age to twenty-one and that educating teens about drinking would be an effective means of addressing their use and abuse of alcohol. Lund asserts that several sound studies clearly show that alcohol-related deaths rise when the drinking age is lowered. In response to the second claim, he says that while educating teens about drinking and driving can be useful, it is insufficient in preventing teens from driving drunk.

In 1972, at a conference on road safety in Canberra, Australia, William Haddon Jr., M.D., the first head of what is now the National Highway Traffic Safety Administration and President of IIHS [Insurance Institute for Highway Safety] from 1969–1985,

Adrian Lund, "Protecting Teens from the Dangers of Alcohol Use and Abuse: Wishful Thinking versus Science," *The Insurance Institute for Highway Safety*, vol. 32, no. 1, October 9, 2007, pp. 10–15. Copyright © 2007 by The Insurance Institute for Highway Safety. All rights reserved.

talked about the beginning of a transition "away from a pre-scientific period. That is, from a period in which folk culture has dominated—in which virtually everyone, both in and out of public life, has been a self-certified expert with his own pet, dogmatically advanced panacea—in which the notion has been virtually absent that public and private conclusions, pronouncements and measures to reduce the losses should be based on well-done, carefully scientific determinations of relevance and efficacy rather than on the unsubstantiated assertions of some individual or group."

This transition to science-based approaches to reducing the deaths and injuries from motor vehicle crashes is not yet complete. Thirty-five years later [in 2007], John M. McCardell, Jr. [vice chancellor of the University of the South and founder of Choose Responsibility] has mounted a campaign to reduce the drinking age from 21 to 18 in the United States. His justification—a desire to reduce the clandestine and sometimes biologically dangerous levels of alcohol consumption among 18–20 year-olds—is laudable. However, his reasoning about what works is quintessentially pre-scientific. Highway safety policies need to be grounded in solid research, not wishful thinking. His arguments are demonstrably wrong. My comments today are limited to his two central theses:

- that the benefits of the 21-year-old drinking age are unproven; and
- that alcohol education for teens promises to be more effective in dealing with the problem of teen alcohol use and abuse.

Both theses are contradicted by fact.

Teen Crashes Vary with Drinking Age Laws

On his website, Mr. McCardell says, "Advocates of the 21-year-old drinking age have long argued that the decrease in fatalities was a result of the lowered drinking age but cannot offer a cause and effect relationship."

That view ignores 30 years of research.

The truth is, the cause and effect are clear. If we lower the drinking age, we will be killing more teens on the highway. Actions among the states in lowering, raising, lowering, and rais-

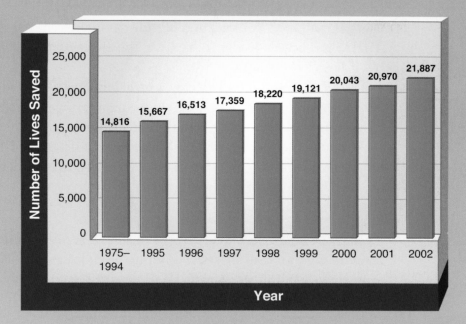

Number of Lives Saved by Minimum Legal Drinking Age Laws Continues to Grow

The chart represents an estimated number of lives saved by minimum legal drinking age laws.

Taken from: John Kindelberger. "Calculating Lives Saved Due to Minimum Drinking Age Laws." NHTSA Traffic Safety Facts, March 2005. www.nrd.nhtsa.dot.gov.

ing again the age at which it is legal to purchase alcohol have provided a series of opportunities to evaluate the effects of these changes on motor vehicle crashes.

In the 1960s and 70s, in the context of the Vietnam war and lowering the voting age to 18, many states also lowered the drinking age from 21 to 18.

IIHS's first study in 1974 looked at two states and one Canadian province that lowered the drinking age, carefully comparing their experience to that of adjacent states that did not change. That study showed that the number of 15–20 year-olds involved in fatal crashes increased in the jurisdictions that lowered the drinking age.

Subsequently, in the late 1970s, states began to increase drinking ages again. Again, it was possible to compare states that made this change to states that didn't. Again, we saw a change related to the drinking age—this time, fatal crash rates declined as teen drinking and teen drinking and driving declined.

IIHS has been a leader in studying the effect of drinking age, but it hasn't been alone.

The CDC [Centers for Disease Control and Prevention] identified many more strong, empirical studies examining the effects of either raising or lowering the minimum drinking age.

Although there's variation the effects are consistent: deaths go up when the drinking age is lowered and they go down when it is raised. The 21-year-old drinking age is saving lives.

Teens participate in a mock traffic accident as part of an educational program on drunk driving. Such programs promise to be more effective in dealing with teen alcohol use and abuse than lowering the drinking age.

Drinking Education Will Not Counteract Easier Availability of Alcohol

While ignoring the vast literature confirming the public health benefit of the 21-year-old minimum drinking age, Mr. McCardell asserts that drinking education could effectively supplant and improve upon 21-year-old drinking laws in combating the problem of alcohol among 18–20 year-olds. What's the evidence?

Mr. McCardell offers none. Nor is there much in the way of evidence about what effect drinking education might have on 18–20 year-olds. However, there is evidence about the effects of driver education, which offers some insights about how drinking education and a drinking license, as recommended by McCardell, might affect teens.

It isn't encouraging.

Again, IIHS has done much of the research on driver education, a fair task since, in years past, much of the funding for driver education in high schools came from insurers. However, when IIHS studied the effects of driver education carefully in the 1970s, a main finding was that teen crashes tended to be higher when high school driver education was available. In the late 1970s, this correlation was confirmed when Connecticut stopped state funding for high school driver education, and many schools in the state dropped the course. The result was fewer teen crashes, based on our study that compared those schools with schools that continued to fund driver education locally.

In response to criticism that these driver education courses were too simplistic, the US DOT [Department of Transportation] spent millions to develop a model course. It was called the Safe Performance Curriculum [SPC] and was submitted to a proper study in DeKalb County, Georgia. When compared to other high school students who received either no driver education or a more basic information course, the result was the same: SPC increased the number of teens getting licensed and the number involved in crashes. This is an unintended consequence of driver education—it can encourage earlier licensure that is not offset by any improvement in knowledge or skill.

Driver education can help drivers learn to operate vehicles and to understand why traffic laws are what they are. Driver education, however, is not itself an effective public health strategy. Drinking education will teach teens about alcohol, but it may only produce better educated drinking and driving teenagers while at the same time making our highways more dangerous. McCardell offers no scientific evidence to the contrary.

Not a Solution

The scientific evidence is clear.

Lowering the legal age to purchase and consume alcohol to 18 would increase the number of 18–20 year-olds killed or injured in motor vehicle crashes.

Others too would die in crashes involving drinking teenagers.

Experience with driver education suggests that drinking education wouldn't counteract this effect. In fact, one implication of driver education experience is that exposing students to drinking education could increase the number drinking. Receiving a license to drink could cause teens and some parents to conclude that the school thinks their teens will drink safely.

This is not the path to reducing the problem of teenage drinking—it is a proven formula for increasing the number of dead teens. Clandestine underage drinking is a problem, but lowering the drinking age is not a solution.

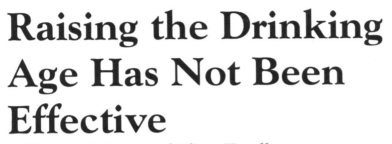

Raising the Drinking Age Has Not Been Effective

Jeffrey A. Miron and Elina Tetelbaum

In the viewpoint below Jeffrey A. Miron, a senior fel-
low at the Cato Institute, and Elina Tetelbaum, a gradu-
ate of Yale University Law School practicing corporate
law, reevaluate the long-accepted view that raising the
drinking age to twenty-one substantially reduced traffic
fatalities. They present their data showing that there was
only a significant drop in traffic fatalities in states that
voluntarily raised the drinking age, and not those that
did so only in response to the 1984 federal law. This suggests that the voluntary states were also engaged in other
efforts to combat alcohol-related deaths, which would
surely contribute to the decrease in deaths. Furthermore,
Miron and Tetelbaum say, both the overall fatality rate
and youth fatality rate have been on a systematic decline
since the 1920s, which might also account for the drop
erroneously credited to the raising of the drinking age.

In 1984, President Ronald Reagan signed the Federal Uniform
Drinking Age Act, a law that threatened to withhold federal
highway funds from states that failed to increase their minimum
legal drinking age (MLDA) to 21. Many states objected to this

Jeffrey A. Miron and Elina Tetelbaum, "Did the Federal Drinking Age Law Save Lives?,"
Regulation—The Cato Institute, Spring 2009, vol. 32, no. 1, Copyright © 2009 by The Cato
Institute. All rights reserved. Reproduced by permission.

federal intrusion and provided for rollback of their MLDA21 if the federal law was repealed or held unconstitutional, or if the federal sanctions expired. South Dakota went so far as to sue Reagan's secretary of transportation, Elizabeth Dole, to prevent implementation of the act. In *South Dakota v. Dole* (1987), however, the U.S. Supreme Court ruled the act constitutional. The Court decided that the "relatively small financial inducement offered by Congress" was not so coercive "as to pass the point at which pressure turns into compulsion." The Court argued, in particular, that promoting "safe interstate travel" was sufficient reason for the federal government to set alcohol policy, a responsibility traditionally reserved to the states under the 21st Amendment.

Research subsequent to the Court's decision appears to confirm that raising the drinking age to 21, and the 1984 federal law in particular, saved lives. Relying on this research, the National Highway Traffic Safety Administration [NHTSA] attributes substantial declines in motor vehicle fatalities to federal and state traffic-safety policies, especially the MLDA21. NHTSA estimates the cumulative number of lives saved by the drinking age law at over 25,000 through 2008. Thus, the conventional view attributes enormous benefit to federal intervention in an area that had traditionally been left to the states.

Voluntary Versus Involuntary Adoption

Our . . . research reexamines whether the 1984 act reduced traffic fatalities by pushing states to adopt a minimum legal drinking age of 21. . . . We compare traffic fatality rates in states before and after they changed their MLDA to 21. . . . We look separately at the effect in states that adopted the higher drinking age on their own versus those pressured to do so by the 1984 law. This is a crucial comparison because the argument for federal imposition rests on the assumption that the act itself reduced fatalities, not just that an MLDA21 reduced fatalities in some states.

The results of our analysis are striking. Virtually all the life-saving effect of the MLDA21 came from a few states that adopted the restriction before the federal law was passed, not from the larger number of states that adopted the restriction under federal pressure. Further, any life-saving effect in the early-adopting states was temporary, occurring largely in the first few years after adoption of the MLDA21. Thus the MLDA21 did not produce its main claimed benefit overall, and any such benefit was in precisely those states where no federal coercion occurred.

Our results therefore challenge the value of coercive federalism. While we cannot rule out a short-term, life-saving effect of the MLDA21 when adopted by states of their own volition, we find no evidence that it saves lives when the federal government compels this policy. This makes sense if a higher MLDA works only when state governments can set a drinking age that reflects local attitudes and concerns, and when states are energized to enforce such laws. A policy imposed from on high—especially one that is readily evaded and opposed by a large fraction of the citizenry—is virtually guaranteed to fail.

Trend Reversal

When the United States repealed Alcohol Prohibition in 1933, the 21st Amendment left states free to legalize, regulate, or prohibit alcohol. Most states chose to legalize but regulate. This new regulation typically included an MLDA, although state reaction to Prohibition's repeal varied. Alabama, for example, maintained state-level prohibition, while Colorado legalized alcohol without adopting a minimum drinking age. Most states set an MLDA between 18 and 21, with 32 adopting an MLDA of 21 and 16 adopting an MLDA between 18 and 20. With few exceptions, those MLDA laws persisted through the late 1960s.

Between 1970 and 1976, 30 states lowered their MLDA from 21 to 18. The policy changes coincided with national efforts toward greater enfranchisement of youth, exemplified by the 26th Amendment granting 18–20 year-olds the right to vote. The reasons for lowering the MLDA are not well understood and may have varied by state. Perhaps the changes reflected Vietnam [War]–era logic that a person old enough to die for America is old enough to drink. Whatever the reasons, the lower MLDAs "enfranchised" over five million 18–20 year-olds to buy alcohol.

Soon after the reductions in the MLDAs, empirical studies claimed that traffic collisions and fatalities were increasing in states that lowered their MLDA, and those findings played a key role in reversing the trend toward lower MLDAs. The justification for the 1984 act, espoused by organizations including the Presidential Commission on Drunk Driving, the American Medical Association, and the National Safety Council, was that higher MLDAs resulted in fewer traffic fatalities among 18–20 year-olds.

Strong Federal Incentive

All states adopted an MLDA21 by the end of 1988. Several states were early adopters (Michigan, Illinois, Maryland, and New Jersey), increasing their MLDAs long before passage of the 1984 act. Other states were less eager to change. For example, Colorado, Iowa, Louisiana, Montana, South Dakota, Texas, and West Virginia passed MLDA21 legislation, but each provided for repeal if the federal law were held unconstitutional. Texas and Kansas enacted "sunset provisions" allowing the MLDA to drop back to previous levels once federal sanctions expired. When the Supreme Court upheld the act's constitutionality, states faced a strong incentive to maintain an MLDA of 21.

Over the past several decades, a large body of literature has examined the effect of the MLDA on traffic fatalities for 18–20 year-olds. This literature concludes that the MLDA21 saves lives and that the federal decision to compel a higher minimum drinking age was instrumental in expanding the benefits of the policy. That conclusion, however, relies on an incomplete examination of the historical record. . . .

The overall fatality rate and the "youth" fatality rate follow similar patterns over the past 90 years [since the 1920s], with both falling systematically over almost the entire period. The similarity in trends fails to suggest a major effect of the 1984 law, since this policy should have affected the 15–24TFR [traffic fatality rate] more than the total TFR.

Although the average MLDA remained at approximately 20 between 1944 and 1970, traffic fatalities decreased substantially

By 1988 all states had adopted a minimum drinking age of twenty-one.

for many years but then increased. In the early 1970s, several states lowered their MLDAs, reducing the average to below 19. A brief increase in traffic fatality rates did occur in the latter half of the 1970s, consistent with prior claims about the MLDA, but the increase looks modest in comparison to the larger downward trend that preceded the changes to the MLDA. Previous studies, which focused on the late 1970s and the early 1980s, were unlikely to see this longstanding trend. In the late 1980s and beyond, when there were no changes in any state's MLDA, the fatality rate continued the same downward trend it displayed during the earlier part of the sample. Overall, the TFR has been decreasing steadily for over 75 years, even though most of the variation in the MLDA occurred in the 1980s. The one major increase in traffic fatalities, from 1961 to 1967, occurred while the average MLDA remained constant.

The key fact, therefore, is that TFRs have been trending downward for decades and display little correlation with changes in the MLDA. This evidence is only suggestive because it does not link fatalities in a given state to MLDA policy in that state. We therefore turn to state-level data.

State-Level Results

In South Carolina, the TFR for 18–20 year-olds was increasing rapidly prior to adoption and then began a marked decline, consistent with an effect of the MLDA21 in reducing fatalities for 18–20 year-olds. In California, however, the TFR for the same age group also declined dramatically, even though the MLDA was 21 throughout. In South Dakota and Louisiana, the TFR for 18–20 year-olds began to decline *prior* to the increase in the MLDA and seems to have decreased at a slower rate after MLDA21 adoption. The [data] . . . for these four states, therefore, show a wide range of "effects" of the MLDA.

This heterogeneity suggests that prior results on the relation between MLDAs and traffic fatalities have been driven by a few states in which the effect is sufficiently negative to outweigh the positive or small effect in most states. The question is whether this heterogeneity is just sampling variation or something more systematic.

Our research shows that the overall negative effect comes from states that adopted the MLDA21 before 1984—that is, before the federal law. . . . The [data] . . . for Michigan and Illinois, two states that adopted an MLDA21 before the 1984 law, appear to show an effect of the MLDA21 in reducing traffic fatalities. . . . [The data] for New York and Texas, two states that were pressured to adopt an MLDA21 by the federal law, suggest no effect of the MLDA21, since fatalities were decreasing before adoption and decreased, if anything, more slowly after adoption. A regression that we conducted . . . confirms that this result is systematic and holds after controlling for other factors that might also affect traffic fatality rates, such as unemployment rates, vehicle miles traveled, per-capita income, and other state alcohol policies.

Thus any effect of the MLDA21 occurred in states where it was adopted endogenously [from within] rather than adopted because of federal pressure. This makes sense, since the MLDA21 in early-adopting states may have been enacted in response to grassroots concern about drunk driving or implemented alongside other efforts to reduce traffic fatalities. Additionally, states that adopted the law on their own may have been states that devoted significant resources to enforcement.

Only Short-Term Effects

Even in the early-adopting states, moreover, the effect of MLDA21 adoption appears to have been transitory rather than long-term. This is apparent from the [data] for Michigan and Illinois . . . , which show that traffic fatalities many years after MLDA21 adoption were not obviously different than implied by the general downward trend that occurred in all states.

The MLDA21 appears to *increase* traffic fatalities among 17-year-old drivers. An explanation for this is that when the MLDA is 18, high school students have access to alcohol through peer networks, including 18-year-olds. When the MLDA is 21, those peer networks are less effective, so individuals younger than 18 feel pressure to drink intensely at each drinking occasion. Alternatively, when the MLDA is 18, law enforcement monitors the drinking behavior of individuals aged 17 and younger. When the MLDA is 21, this monitoring is spread more thinly, resulting in more drinking among 17-year-olds. Still further, teenagers might care both about respecting the law and about how long they must postpone drinking in order to comply with the law. If the drinking age is 18, 17-year-olds know they can obey the law by postponing for only one year, and some choose that path. If the drinking age is 21, however, 17-year-olds know they have to postpone drinking for four years to comply with the law, so more decide to become law-breakers.

The bottom line, therefore, is that neither the increases in the MLDA caused by the 1984 law, nor the MLDA21 generally, has had a significant life-saving effect. Indeed, the results for 17-year-olds suggest this policy may actually be counterproductive.

An Ongoing Debate

Whether government policy should be set at the state or federal level is the subject of ongoing debate. The main argument for federal intervention is that leaving policy choices to states permits a "race to the bottom" in which states choose insufficient regulation, such as lax pollution controls, for fear of driving away business. A different argument for federal regulation is avoidance of conflicting or varied regulation across states that might burden businesses or confuse consumers.

The main argument for state-level policymaking is that economic and social problems vary in their nature and intensity from state to state, so the appropriate policy should also vary. States with little industry, for example, might have less reason to limit air pollution than their more densely populated neighbors. States with wide-open highways can allow higher speed limits without generating large numbers of traffic accidents. State-level policymaking is also desirable if political forces cause some interventions to expand excessively. In this case, the race to the bottom counters a different tendency toward overexpansion.

Advocates of state-level policies also note that, in practice, states do not consistently choose as little regulation or redistribution as possible. Several states have minimum wages or unemployment insurance benefits at levels above the federal standard, just as several states, like California, have stricter pollution regula-

Population change and drunk driving fatalities:

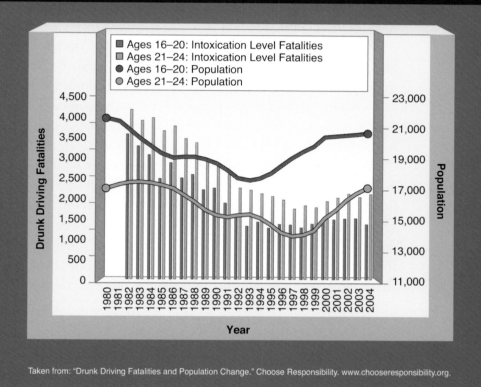

Taken from: "Drunk Driving Fatalities and Population Change." Choose Responsibility. www.chooseresponsibility.org.

tion. Many state constitutions go beyond the U.S. Constitution in protecting individual liberties, such as Connecticut's guarantee for public education and South Carolina's commitment to public court proceedings In the 1920s and 1930s, more than 30 states adopted Social Security programs even at the risk of attracting recipients from other states. Thus, states may be willing to bear the costs of regulation or redistribution out of altruism or public spiritedness.

It is thus an empirical question as to whether state versus federal regulation is preferable, and the right answer presumably differs to some degree across policies (e.g., national defense versus education). We have challenged here the notion that the drinking age needs to be legislated federally, arguing that federal pressure for states to adopt an MLDA21 did not save lives as has previously been suggested.

The general trend in the United States, however, has been toward an expanded federal role. The extent of legitimate federal regulation is inextricably linked to the U.S. Supreme Court's jurisprudence on the Interstate Commerce Clause. As described in *Gonzales v. Raich* (2005), "Interpretation of the sixteen words of the Commerce Clause has helped define the balance of power between the federal government and the states. . . . As such, it has a direct impact on the lives of American citizens." While the outer limits of the Commerce Clause power will be shaped, in part, by the future appointments to the Supreme Court, the debate will also be informed by empirical analyses of just how substantially related to interstate commerce a proposed federal policy is. Where the Commerce Clause fails to legitimize federal intervention into state policy, the taxing and spending power that saved the 1984 act may become the favored mechanism to compel policies across states.

The Ineffectiveness of Coercive Federalism

Thus in challenging the effectiveness of the federal drinking age law, our results challenge the value of coercive federalism. The case of the drinking age law informs several other public policy debates, including the appropriateness of the 2001 No Child Left Behind Act (NCLB). When Utah's governor attempted to ignore NCLB provisions that conflicted with Utah's own education policy, the Department of Education threatened to withhold federal education funding. In a 2005 *Peabody Journal of Education* paper, Lance Fusarelli argues that such actions demonstrate that in just "a few short years, federal education policy had shifted from minimal federal involvement (President Reagan wanted to abolish the U.S. Department of Education) to the development of voluntary national standards (under President [Bill] Clinton) to the new law mandating testing of all students in Grades 3–8." The empirical strategy employed in our work might tease out whether the successes attributed to the NCLB are similarly driven by states that proactively adopted education reforms prior to the federal mandate.

Additionally, this empirical approach might help establish whether other federal policies promote "the general welfare" enough to satisfy the *South Dakota v. Dole* restrictions on when Congress can condition funding for states. If the case of the Federal Uniform Drinking Age Act is any indication, the federal government may at times be working against its own policy objectives and against the general welfare.

What You Should Know About Drunk Driving

Demographics of Drunk Drivers

According to the Century Council:

- The number of women arrested for driving while intoxicated (DWI) in the United States increased by 29 percent from 1997 to 2007.
- Three percent of drivers involved in fatal crashes in the United States in 2010 had a prior DWI conviction within the past three years.

The Insurance Institute for Highway Safety reports:

- Among fatally injured passenger vehicle drivers in the United States in 2010, a higher proportion of males than females had a blood alcohol concentration (BAC) at or above 0.08 percent at every age.
- In 2010 the age group in the United States with the lowest rate of fatally injured drivers with a BAC of 0.08 percent or higher was seventy and older.
- In 2010, 29 percent of fatally injured drivers in the United States with BACs at or above 0.15 percent were male, and 16 percent were female.

According to the Centers for Disease Control and Prevention (CDC):

- An average drunk driver in the United States has driven drunk eighty times before his or her first arrest.

- Men were responsible for four in five episodes (81 percent) of drinking and driving in the United States in 2010.

According to the Substance Abuse and Mental Health Services Administration:
- In 2011 males in the United States were more likely than females to drive under the influence of alcohol (15.1 percent versus 7.9 percent).
- In 2008 the age group in the United States with the highest rate of driving under the influence of alcohol was twenty-one- to twenty-five-year-olds.

Alcohol and Young Drivers

The Higher Education Center for Alcohol, Drug Abuse, and Violence Prevention states:
- Eleven hundred of the fourteen hundred alcohol-related college student deaths in the United States per year involve drinking and driving.
- Thirty percent of college students in the United States who drank said they drove after drinking in the previous thirty days.

According to the CDC:
- The percentage of US teens in high school who drink and drive has decreased by more than half since 1991.
- Nearly 1 million US high school teens drank alcohol and got behind the wheel in 2011.
- Teen drivers in the United States are three times more likely than more experienced drivers to be in a fatal crash.

The CDC's 2011 Youth Risk Behavior Survey found that among US high school students in the past thirty days:
- Thirty-nine percent had drunk some amount of alcohol.
- Eight percent had driven after drinking alcohol.
- Twenty-four percent had ridden with a driver who had been drinking alcohol.

Alcohol-Related Traffic Accidents

According to the Advocates for Highway and Auto Safety:

- Three in every ten Americans will be involved in an alcohol-related crash at some point in their lifetime.
- In 2008, 37,261 people were killed in motor vehicle crashes in the United States, and 11,773, or 32 percent, of these were alcohol related.
- In 2008, 16 percent of the children aged fourteen and younger who were killed in motor vehicle crashes in the United States died in alcohol-related crashes.

The National Highway Traffic Safety Administration reports that in the United States:

- Almost every ninety seconds, a person is injured in a drunk driving crash.
- On average, someone is killed by a drunk driver every fifty-two minutes.
- In 2010, 16 percent of all drivers involved in fatal crashes during the week were alcohol impaired, compared to 31 percent on weekends.
- The rate of fatal crashes related to alcohol use is four times higher at night than during the day.

According to the Century Council, in the United States:

- The rate of alcohol-impaired driving fatalities decreased 64 percent from 1982 to 2010.
- Alcohol-impaired driving fatalities accounted for 31 percent of the total vehicle traffic fatalities in 2010.
- Between 1991 and 2010 the rate of drunk driving fatalities per one hundred thousand people decreased 48 percent nationally and 63 percent among those under age twenty-one.

Drunk Driving Laws and Penalties

The Governors Highway Safety Association states:

- In all fifty US states, it is illegal for a person to drive when his or her BAC level reaches 0.08 percent.

- Forty-eight US states and the District of Columbia have increased penalties for drunk drivers found guilty of driving with a high BAC (often 0.15 or higher).

According to the Insurance Institute for Highway Safety:
- Forty-one US states and the District of Columbia have administrative license suspension laws, but the laws vary with regard to the length of suspension.
- Administrative license suspension laws have been found to reduce the number of drivers involved in fatal crashes by about 9 percent during nighttime hours in the United States.
- More than half of all US states require DWI offenders to install ignition interlocks on their vehicles for specified time periods before fully relicensing offenders.
- An estimated 249,000 ignition interlocks were in use in 2011 in the United States.
- In all fifty US states, drivers younger than age twenty-one are prohibited from operating a vehicle with any detectable blood alcohol, defined in most states as a BAC at or above 0.02 percent.
- Sobriety checkpoints are prohibited in ten US states.

What You Should Do About Drunk Driving

At first glance, drunk driving seems like a nondebatable issue. After all, no one is in favor of drunk driving, right? While it is true that most, if not all, people agree that drunk driving should be stopped, there is widespread disagreement about how best to prevent it. While many drunk driving activists focus on legislative means of prevention, drunk driving is a social issue—and as such, there is a lot that you can do to influence the attitudes and behavior of those around you and hopefully lead to more enlightened decisions about alcohol use.

Research the Topic

Most people know that they should not drink and drive. They have heard the public service announcements, seen the TV advertisements, and listened to lectures in their classrooms. But few people really know *why*. That is, how exactly does alcohol impair a person's ability to drive an automobile?

You may have heard that alcohol impairs judgment, but this may sound a bit vague or abstract. There are a lot of sources out there—books, periodical articles, websites—that explain the effects of alcohol on the brain in ways nonbiologists can understand. Find out, for instance, which parts of the brain are affected by alcohol, to what extent, and what these effects look like in the brain of a driver. For instance, alcohol decreases activity in the prefrontal cortex, the part of the brain responsible for rational thought and decision making. Knowing this kind of particular information often proves more persuasive than just "don't drink and drive" when you are trying to make a decision—or influence someone else's decision—regarding alcohol use.

Make a Plan for Getting Home Safely

When you go out with friends to an event or location where you know there will be alcohol, you should always collectively decide on a "designated driver" ahead of time. A designated driver is a person who agrees to refrain from drinking alcohol throughout the *entire* course of the event. This way, the rest of the group can be reassured that they will have a safe ride home. In many social groups, individuals alternate taking on the designated driver role. But when it is your turn, it is crucial that you do what you agreed to do, just as you would expect your peers to do for you.

Just in case your designated driver does not hold up his or her end of the bargain, you should have a "plan B" in place for getting yourself home; *do not* get into the car with this person. If you have older siblings, it might be wise to ask them if they would be willing to pick you up. Although you may be reluctant to call your parents because you are afraid they will scold you for going someplace where alcohol is present, know that most parents will in fact be happy that you called them to ask for a ride instead of putting yourself in danger. There are also a growing number of companies, nonprofit organizations, restaurants, bars, universities, and municipalities with "designated driver services" that will pick you up and drive you home, usually for a low cost, and sometimes for free. Even if you cannot imagine ever needing such a service, it would still be wise to find a few offered in your community and keep their phone numbers with you.

Encourage Others to Use Alcohol Wisely

While your primary concern should be your own safety, this does not mean you should turn a blind eye to someone else making unwise decisions. Just as you might make an agreement with a sibling to give you a ride if your designated driver is drunk, it is a good idea to talk with a friend (or two) before you arrive at a situation involving alcohol and agree to look out for each other. At the very least, make a vow to check in with each other before either of you leaves. If your friend is getting a ride from someone who has been drinking, let your friend know and help him or her find an alternative. Or if your friend is climbing into her own driver's seat and slurring her words, intervene and tell her you will help her find an alternative.

Many young people do not want to be "that guy" at the party who tells someone that he or she is too drunk to drive, because they fear the driver will react with hostility or that they will be teased. But keep in mind that the drunk person is currently not thinking clearly and, in fact, when he or she reflects on the incident (sometime the next morning), the person will probably look upon the whole thing with an entirely different perspective and feel grateful to the friend who stepped in. In the clear light of day, the person who was called a "wuss" or "goody-goody" the night before now appears to be the gutsy one.

Help Raise Awareness in Your School or Community

Now that you know more about drunk driving, you are better equipped to make good choices for yourself and help others do so as well. But why stop there? You can have an even bigger impact on reducing drunk driving by raising awareness on a larger scale, like at your school or in your community at large. You might consider starting a local chapter of a national organization, such as Students Against Destructive Decisions (SADD). When you become affiliated with a larger organization, it can be easier to educate and empower your peers because much of the infrastructure—literature, speakers, activities, etc.—for your organization will already be in place.

If you would prefer to start your own group focused on reducing drunk driving, there are many ways to do this as well. You might start by bringing a speaker to your community who will bring attention to the problem. Another strategy that many student organizations use is to display a "mock car crash" that shows the damage that can be done when one or more drivers has been drinking. Whichever tactic you use, once you feel you have demonstrated the seriousness of drunk driving, gather together those who seem to want to do something about the problem and discuss ways that you can do this. After all, a problem that has so many causes and effects has at least as many solutions.

The editors have compiled the following list of organizations concerned with the issues debated in this book. The descriptions are derived from materials provided by the organizations. All have publications or information available for interested readers. The list was compiled on the date of publication of the present volume; names, addresses, phone and fax numbers, and e-mail and Internet addresses may change. Be aware that many organizations take several weeks or longer to respond to inquiries, so allow as much time as possible.

Advocates for Highway and Auto Safety
750 First St. NE, Ste. 901
Washington, DC 20002
(202) 408-1711
fax: (202) 408-1699
e-mail: advocates@saferoads.org
website: www.saferoads.org

Advocates for Highway and Auto Safety is an organization made up of consumer, health, and safety groups and insurance companies dedicated to improving the safety of America's roads through federal and state legislation, policies, and programs. The organization focuses on safety belt use, speeding, motorcycle helmets, and impaired driving. The group publishes an annual *Roadmap to State Safety Laws*.

Centers for Disease Control and Prevention (CDC)
1600 Clifton Rd.
Atlanta, GA 30333
(800) 232-4636
e-mail: cdcinfo@cdc.gov
website: www.cdc.gov

The CDC is a government agency aimed at promoting health; preventing disease, injury, and disability; and preparing for threats to public health. The CDC's work addresses numerous issues, among them seat belt use, binge drinking, and drinking and driving. Its publications include issue-specific journals, weekly reports, fact sheets, and many others.

Century Council
2345 Crystal Dr., Ste. 710
Arlington, VA 22202
(202) 637-0077
fax: (202) 637-0079
website: www.centurycouncil.org

The Century Council is a national not-for-profit organization of distillers aimed at promoting responsible decision making regarding alcoholic beverage consumption. Its work focuses on issues of drunk driving, underage drinking, and binge drinking. The Century Council publishes a multitude of guides on these issues, such as the *2010 State of Drunk Driving Fatalities in America*, *Combating Hardcore Drunk Driving Sourcebook*, and *Ignition Interlocks: What You Should Know*.

Governors Highway Safety Association (GHSA)
444 N. Capitol St. NW, Ste. 722
Washington, DC 20001-1534
(202) 789-0942
fax: (202) 789-0946
e-mail: headquarters@ghsa.org
website: www.ghsa.org

The GHSA provides leadership and advocacy for state and territorial highway safety offices with the goal of improving traffic safety. The GHSA addresses behavioral highway safety issues such as impaired driving and speeding. It publishes the newsletter *Directions in Highway Safety*, legislative advocacy guides, and community guides for preventing underage drinking.

Insurance Institute for Highway Safety
1005 N. Glebe Rd., Ste. 800
Arlington, VA 22201
(703) 247-1500
fax: (703) 247-1588
website: www.iihs.org

The Insurance Institute for Highway Safety is a nonprofit scientific and educational organization supported by automobile insurers with the goal of reducing deaths, injuries, and property damage from crashes on the nation's roads. Among its policy areas are roadside hazards, safety belt use, and alcohol/drugs and driving. The institute publishes the newsletter *Status Report*, in-depth research reports, and consumer guides such as *Beginning Teenage Drivers*.

International Center for Alcohol Policies (ICAP)
1519 New Hampshire Ave. NW
Washington, DC 20036
(202) 986-1159
fax: (202) 986-2080
e-mail: info@icap.org
website: www.icap.org

The ICAP is a not-for-profit organization sponsored by leading alcoholic beverage producers that is dedicated to promoting the understanding of the role of alcohol in society and reducing alcohol abuse worldwide. The ICAP focuses on alcohol policies across the world, drunk driving, young people and drinking, alcohol marketing, and other issues. The organization's publications include a book series on alcohol and society, comparative alcohol policy analyses, and reviews of alcohol issues, among others.

Mothers Against Drunk Driving (MADD)
511 E. John Carpenter Fwy., Ste. 700
Irving, TX 75062
(877) 275-6233
fax: (972) 869-2206 or (972) 869-2207
website: www.madd.org

MADD is a nonprofit organization devoted to stopping drunk driving, supporting the victims of drunk driving, and preventing underage drinking. MADD advocates for policy changes, educates the public, and provides victim services. Among its publications are fact sheets, the monthly e-newsletter *MADD Messenger*, and the biannual publication *MADDvocate*.

National Conference of State Legislatures (NCSL)

444 N. Capitol St. NW, Ste. 515
Washington, DC 20001
(202) 624-5400
fax: (202) 737-1069

The NCSL is a bipartisan organization providing resources to the legislators and staffs of all fifty states and advocating for the interests of state governments. The NCSL focuses on numerous issue areas, including transportation issues such as bicycles and pedestrians, driver's licensing and registration, and impaired driving. Publications of the NCSL include the monthly *NCSL Transport Report Newsletter*, *LegisBriefs* such as *Impaired Driving and Ignition Interlock Laws*, and many others.

National Highway Traffic Safety Administration (NHTSA)

1200 New Jersey Ave. SE, West Building
Washington, DC 20590
(888) 327-4236
website: www.nhtsa.gov

The NHTSA is dedicated to motor vehicle and highway safety and strives to prevent crashes and their human and financial costs. The NHTSA's areas of concern include driving safety issues like distracted driving and impaired driving, as well as vehicle safety issues like air bags, recalls, and defects. Its publications include *A Guide for Local Impaired-Driving Task Forces*, a *Community How-To Guide on Underage Drinking Prevention*, and various case study reports.

National Institute on Alcohol Abuse and Alcoholism (NIAAA)
National Institutes of Health
Building 1, 1 Center Dr.
Bethesda, MD 20892
(888) 696-4222
website: www.niaaa.nih.gov

The NIAAA, a part of the National Institutes of Health, supports and conducts research on the impact of alcohol consumption on health and supports prevention and treatment of alcohol-related problems. The NIAAA's research initiatives include development of treatments for alcoholism, underage and college drinking, and fetal alcohol spectrum disorders. The institute's publications include the quarterly bulletin *Alcohol Alert*, the *NIAAA Spectrum* webzine, and various brochures and fact sheets.

National Motorists Association (NMA)
402 W. Second St.
Waunakee, WI 53597
(608) 849-6000
fax: (608) 849-8697
website: www.motorists.org

The NMA is a driver advocacy organization promoting fairness in traffic laws, enforcement, and penalties. Its areas of focus include speed limits, driving under the influence (DUI)/driving while intoxicated (DWI) regulations, and auto insurance laws. The NMA publishes a blog, a weekly e-newsletter, *Driving Freedoms* magazine, and various fact sheets.

National Youth Rights Association (NYRA)
1101 Fifteenth St. NW, Ste. 200
Washington, DC 20005
(202) 835-1719
website: www.youthrights.org

The NYRA is a nonprofit organization devoted to protecting the civil and human rights of young people in the United States. Its primary issues are the drinking age, voting age, and curfew laws. The NYRA's publications include the *NYRA Chapter Handbook*, *Students Rights Handbook*, and a number of flyers with information on these issues.

Students Against Destructive Decisions (SADD)
255 Main St.
Marlborough, MA 01752
(877) 723-3462
fax: (508) 481-5759
e-mail: info@sadd.org
website: http://sadd.org

SADD is a peer-to-peer educational and advocacy organization. Its work focuses on preventing young people from making destructive decisions, particularly underage drinking and risky and impaired driving. Among its publications are two e-newsletters, the *SADDvocate* and *ParentTeen Matters*.

Traffic Injury Research Foundation (TIRF)
171 Nepean St., Ste. 200
Ottawa, ON
Canada K2P 0B4
(613) 238-5235
fax: (613) 238-5292
e-mail: tirf@tirf.ca
website: www.tirf.ca

The TIRF is Canada's primary road safety research institute, providing information to government, industry, nongovernmental organizations, and the public. It focuses on issues related to road users such as pedestrians and senior drivers, driver behavior such as speeding and alcohol-impaired driving, and countermeasures such as driver education and alcohol interlock devices. Among its publications are *Fatigued Driving Fast Facts*, the annual *Canadian Motor Vehicle Traffic Collisions Statistics*, and *DWI System Improvements for Dealing with Hard Core Drunk Drivers*.

United Nations Road Safety Collaboration
World Health Organization
Avenue Appia 20
1211 Geneva 27
Switzerland
+41 22 791 21 11
fax: +41 22 791 3 11
website: www.who.int/roadsafety/en

The United Nations Road Safety Collaboration, coordinated by the World Health Organization, is a mechanism designed to implement United Nations recommendations regarding traffic injury prevention and to facilitate international cooperation toward improving global road safety. The collaboration has published *Advocating for Road Safety and Road Traffic Injury Victims: A Guide for Nongovernmental Organizations*; *Drinking and Driving: A Road Safety Manual for Decision-Makers and Practitioners*; and the newsletter *The Road Ahead*, among others.

BIBLIOGRAPHY

Books

Dennis A. Bjorklund, *Drunk Driving/DUI: A Survival Guide for Motorists*. San Francisco: Praetorian, 2011.

Dennis A. Bjorklund, *Drunk Driving Laws: Rules of the Road When Crossing State Lines*. 2nd ed. San Francisco: Praetorian, 2010.

James M. Byrne and Donald J. Repovich, eds., *The New Technology of Crime, Law and Social Control*. Monsey, NY: Criminal Justice, 2007.

Amitava Dasgupta, *The Science of Drinking: How Alcohol Affects Your Body and Mind*. Lanham, MD: Rowman & Littlefield, 2011.

David Edvin and Samuel Harald, *Underage Drinking: Examining and Preventing Youth Use of Alcohol*. Hauppauge, NY: Nova Science, 2010.

Steve Fox, Paul Armentano, and Mason Tvert, *Marijuana Is Safer: So Why Are We Driving People to Drink?* White River Junction, VT: Chelsea Green, 2009.

Anthony F. Jones, *Alcohol-Impaired Drivers Detection Technology*. Hauppauge, NY: Nova Science, 2011.

Steven B. Karch, ed., *Forensic Issues in Alcohol Testing*. Boca Raton, FL: CRC, 2007.

Barron H. Lerner, *One for the Road: Drunk Driving Since 1900*. Baltimore: Johns Hopkins University Press, 2011.

Maria T. Schulteis, John DeLuca, and Douglas Chute, eds., *Handbook for the Assessment of Driving Capacity*. New York: Academic, 2008.

Joris C. Verster, S.R. Pandi-Perumal, Jan G. Ramaekers, and Johan J. de Gier, eds., *Drugs, Driving and Traffic Safety*. Basel, Switzerland: Birkhauser, 2008.

Periodicals and Internet Sources

Peter Applebome, "A Dead End in Eradicating Drunk Driving," *New York Times*, September 21, 2009.

John Cloud, "Should the Drinking Age Be Lowered?," *Time*, June 6, 2008.

Philip J. Cook and Maeve E. Gearing, "The Breathalyzer Behind the Wheel," *New York Times*, August 31, 2009.

Larry Copeland, "Sobriety Checkpoints Open to Controversy," *USA Today*, March 24, 2011.

Bob Dyer, "Sobriety Checkpoints Are Intrusive and Ineffective," *Akron (OH) Beacon Journal*, October 2, 2007.

Deborah A. Garbato, "Not a One-Shot Deal: Effective Training Must Be Thorough and Ongoing," *Cheers*, September 2009.

Jonathon Gatehouse, "Curbing Drunk Drivers Is Harder than You Think," *Maclean's*, December 14, 2009.

Abby Goodnough, "Fatal Accident Puts Focus on Deportation Program," *New York Times*, September 30, 2011.

Michele Grayson, "Locking In on Interlock," *Cheers*, July–August 2009.

Valerie Schremp Hahn, "Social Media Users Get the Word Out About Sobriety Checkpoints," *St. Louis (MO) Post-Dispatch*, March 17, 2012.

David Harsanyi, "Prohibition Returns! Teetotaling Do-Gooders Attack Your Right to Drink," *Reason*, November 2007.

Nicholas Kohler, Michael Friscolanti, and Stephanie Findlay, "A Life Lost and a Life Destroyed," *Maclean's*, January 17, 2011.

Anna Kordunsky, "Tougher Penalties Sought in Russia for Drunken Driving After Accident," *New York Times*, September 26, 2012.

Katherine Mangu-Ward, "Scared Sober: Another Way to Waste Taxpayers' Money and Schoolchildren's Time," *Weekly Standard*, August 4, 2008.

Toben F. Nelson and Traci L. Toomey, "Drinking Age of 21 Saves Lives," *CNN*, September 29, 2009. http://edition.cnn.com/2009/US/09/29/nelson.retain.drinking.age/index.html.

New York Times, "Fewer Teenagers Are Driving After Drinking, Study Shows," October 3, 2012.

Michelle Perin, "Police Supporting High School Drunk Driving Educational Programs," *Officer*, April 2012. www.officer.com/article/10704859/police-supporting-high-school-drunk-driving-educational-programs.

Michael L. Rich, "The Perfect Non-Crime," *New York Times*, August 7, 2012.

Katie Rooney, "Revoking Licenses Deters Drunk Driving," *Time*, July 25, 2007.

William Saletan, "Mad at MADD," *Slate*, August 29, 2011. www.slate.com/articles/health_and_science/human_nature/2011/08/mad_at_madd.html.

Randall Stross, "Helping Drunken Drivers Avoid Tickets, but Not Wrecks," *New York Times*, April 17, 2011.

Bethany Vaccaro, "'I Drove Drunk and Killed Two Sisters,'" *Glamour*, February 2011.